I0031960

The International Library of Sociology

YOUTH AND THE SOCIAL ORDER

Founded by KARL MANNHEIM

The International Library of Sociology

THE SOCIOLOGY OF YOUTH AND ADOLESCENCE
In 12 Volumes

YOUTH AND THE SOCIAL ORDER

by

F. MUSGROVE

Routledge
Taylor & Francis Group

LONDON AND NEW YORK

First published in 1964
by Routledge

Reprinted in 1998, 2000, 2002
by Routledge
2 Park Square, Milton Park, Abingdon, Oxon, OX14 4RN

711 Third Avenue, New York, NY 10017

Transferred to Digital Printing 2007

Routledge is an imprint of the Taylor & Francis Group

First issued in paperback 2013

© 1964 F. Musgrove

All rights reserved. No part of this book may be reprinted or reproduced
or utilized in any form or by any electronic, mechanical, or other means,
now known or hereafter invented, including photocopying
and recording, or in any information storage or retrieval system, without
permission in writing from the publishers.

The publishers have made every effort to contact authors/copyright holders
of the works reprinted in *The International Library of Sociology*.
This has not been possible in every case, however, and we would
welcome correspondence from those individuals/companies
we have been unable to trace.

British Library Cataloguing in Publication Data
A CIP catalogue record for this book
is available from the British Library

ISBN13: 978-0-415-17672-9 (hbk)

ISBN13: 978-0-415-86354-4 (pbk)

Publisher's Note
The publisher has gone to great lengths to ensure the quality
of this reprint but points out that some imperfections
in the original may be apparent

CONTENTS

v

Contents

TABLES

vii

ACKNOWLEDGEMENTS

CHAPTERS four, five and six are based on articles which the author has published in *The Sociological Review, The British Journal of Social and Clinical Psychology* and *The British Journal of Educational Psychology* respectively. He thanks the editors of these journals for permission to use the material in this book.

Chapter One

INTRODUCTION

THE central concern of this book is the status of youth, its determinants and consequences. This is necessarily an inter-disciplinary study, for no single intellectual discipline or method of inquiry could deal effectively with the range of argument and evidence which must be assembled and reviewed.

The present status of the young can be seen emerging from the economic, demographic and educational changes of the past century—as well as from changing values in part determined by new philosophies and psychologies. The status of the young has profound consequences for the kind and quality of relationship which exists between the generations; it is related to the enterprise and inventiveness which a nation shows, to the tempo of social change. The differences in status between various groups of young people, which arise very largely from their economic functions and the type of education they enjoy, have a bearing on the way in which they relate themselves to wider society: these status differences underlie such varying responses as delinquency, separatist cultural or political youth movements, or apathetic conformity to the prevailing values of the adult world.

A great output of books and research papers in recent decades bears witness to 'the problem of youth' today. Some years of experience of English educational institutions and of the position of the young in the rapidly changing tribal societies of Africa led the author to the conclusion that the issues of status had been insufficiently explored in the extensive literature which deals with the young. Role has been analyzed without sufficient attention to the underlying status which helps to explain it (with the notable exception of 'subcultural' interpretations of delinquency).

The author made a first brief and tentative statement of this view in an essay which appeared in 1958.[1] While some of the emphases and suggestions of this essay have been modified in the light of further study and research, this essay of five years ago was the point of departure for a programme of investigation, and substantially foreshadows the main lines of the present book.

Four major assumptions which are commonly made about the place of youth in modern society seemed to the author to merit special attention. The view that the status of youth tends to improve when young people are extensively excluded ('protected') from the nation's economic life and undergo a more prolonged formal education, seemed over-simple. An examination of the changing status of the young over the past century or so in the light of their importance to the economy and the educational provision made for them, might be expected to throw some light on this problem. The truth appears to be much more complicated; for their exclusion from employment may seriously undermine their social power.

The segregation of the young from the world of their seniors has given them a special position in society. In some respects it is a position of diminished rather than enhanced social status. While demographic changes—the supply of young human beings—and economic developments are in large measure responsible for this segregation, psychological theories about the nature of youth have helped to justify it. The position of youth in contemporary society is only intelligible in terms of the rise since the later eighteenth century of a psychology of adolescence which has helped to create what it describes.

A second common assumption today is that young people have widely rejected the standards, guidance and authority of their seniors and are even united in hostility towards them. This hypothesis could only be tested by using the survey techniques of the social psychologist and investigating the attitudes of samples of young people towards adults, and of adults towards young people. The 'rejection' by the young of their elders was a more complicated phenomenon, and far less extreme, than had been supposed. (See Chapter Five.) What emerged with the greatest clarity was the rejection of the young by adults.

The importance of youth to a society is often held to lie in its

[1] See F. Musgrove, 'Adolescent Status. Rights Withheld Too Long', *The Times Educational Supplement* (24 October 1958).

vigorous inventiveness, its willingness to experiment and to consider new ideas. The behaviour of the generality of young people in post-war Britain (with the exception of a few notable but very small minorities) did not seem to support this view. But the idea was tested by making a comparative or 'cross-cultural' study of a wide variety of societies for which relevant data existed. This anthropological approach (Chapter Seven) yielded results which, while they may not be conclusive, are highly suggestive. There are indications from many contrasted societies that youth will provide an impetus towards social experimentation and change not when they are given power but when they are denied it. The will to experiment is closely related to the status of the experimenters, but perhaps in a contrary fashion to what is commonly supposed.

Historical, sociological and anthropological methods and materials seemed appropriate to these three major problems concerning youth's relationship to wider society. The fourth problem, of the consequences of differences in status among the young themselves, called for some of the techniques of the psychologist.

There is an idea which has widespread credence, that today, quite apart from questions of birth, our educational system selects a 'privileged'—or anyway a highly favoured—minority and leaves the great bulk of young people with a sense of failure, rejection, and resentment. These two broad groups might be expected to see themselves differently, and to relate themselves differently to wider social life, because of their differences in status.

It was the inquiry (Chapter Six) designed to test the truth of this view which produced some of the most unexpected, indeed startling and disconcerting, results. The psychological tests which were devised to compare the way in which 'selected' and 'unselected' adolescents saw themselves and their society showed conflicts among grammar-school pupils which would scarcely be expected among a favoured, high-status minority. Far from feeling at one with a beneficent world, they appeared beset by irreconcilable social demands. The 'rejected', the 'failures' in the modern schools, seemed to suffer far less doubt and uncertainty, and to identify themselves far more closely with the adult world.

These findings are, in a general sense, congruent with other work on the attitudes and characteristics of students in our selective educational institutions. And they provide ground for profound disquiet. So important do these results seem to the author, and so disastrous their wider social implications, that he proposes in concluding this Introduction to bring this general issue firmly to the fore.

The phenomenon of high 'role-conflict' among grammar-school pupils, which is reported in Chapter Six, is interpreted chiefly in terms of the social pressures and tensions which the latter experience in some measure out of school, but principally within it. Characteristically the English grammar school humiliates most those it serves best. It firmly insists that they 'keep their place' in return for the services it renders. An institution which confers or at least promises high status, it will tolerate no touch of arrogance—or even proper cheerful self-expression—in its pupils.

But it can probably reduce the majority of its pupils to a seemly subservience and state of self-doubt all the more effectively because the pupils perhaps tend, in a general way, to be of a personality type which makes this relatively easy. Institutions which were not concerned to exploit their deficiencies (which are in some sense their strength) would not have the same effect.

We have fashioned institutions of higher education which can achieve their ends most easily with a certain personality type: which can relatively easily be made to feel guilt and self-reproach and to drive itself without overmuch steering. This type of person is characterized by what Eysenck has described as the introverted and neurotic 'dimensions of personality'.[1] He is rewarded for, and confirmed in, these particular dimensions. Individuals who are stable and extravert seem to do less well in the activities which are valued by grammar schools and universities, even though they are of similar intelligence.[2] (It is not a matter of 'intelligence': there is no question of high introversion or neuroticism necessarily connoting high intelligence as measured by intelligence tests.) And particularly at the borderline of

[1] See H. J. Eysenck, *The Scientific Study of Personality* (1952).
[2] For evidence on introversion among the more successful Cambridge students see D. E. Broadbent, *Perception and Communication* (1958), ch. 7.

university admission extraverts probably tend more often than introverts to be denied a place.[1]

It has been suggested that extraversion is not in itself a handicap in academic pursuits below the level of university education, but there is evidence that our present system is already penalizing the (intelligent) extravert before this stage.[2] Any human society is highly selective of those aspects of human activity and achievement which its educational system takes seriously into account. Our own system is almost exclusively concerned with those activities and exercises in which 'neurotic introverts' tend to excel. Unfortunately their excellence in these matters is thought to qualify them for future roles for which they may be quite unsuited.[3]

Our emphasis in higher education is on a narrow range of a persons's capacities and possibilities. These have the advantage of being fairly easily assessed. Other societies place their emphasis differently. The society which produced the *Kama Sutra* (like Aldous Huxley's fictional island of Pala[4]) would take into account in its educational provision aspects of the human personality and capacity for experience which we have chosen to ignore or regret.

Our formal educational system concerns itself with a highly selective range of human attributes which receive attention because of tradition and the pressures of contemporary social and economic circumstances. Of central concern are written-verbal skills and extended preparation for their assessment. (Oral-verbal skills have no such prominence. It is still possible to pass with distinction through many an English grammar school—and through some courses in some of our universities—virtually without speaking; indeed, overmuch speaking, however much to the point, would make a distinguished grammar-school career highly unlikely.)

[1] See W. D. Furneaux, 'The Psychologist and the University', *Universities Quarterly* (1962), **17**. Thus 25·7 per cent of a borderline group of applicants for an engineering department were 'neurotic extraverts', but neurotic extraverts were only 6·2 per cent of those from this group who were admitted. The proportions of 'neurotic introverts' were 21·4 per cent and 37·5 per cent respectively.

[2] See R. Lynn, 'Two Personality Characteristics Related to Academic Achievement', *British Journal of Educational Psychology* (1959), **29**.

[3] For a full examination of the vulnerability of this personality in some of the circumstances of modern professional life see the author's book, *The Migratory Élite* (1963), particularly ch. 7.

[4] Aldous Huxley, *Island* (1962).

In many other societies this is not so. Nor was it with us when the *viva voce* examination figured far more prominently in the examination of students. The Nyakyusa of Tanganyika place emphasis in their educational procedures on *oral*-verbal skills, the ability to communicate effectively with one's fellows through the spoken word. It is perhaps a corollary that they prize most highly the virtues of comradeship and the arts of social intercourse.[1]

There may be some doubt about the effectiveness of anxiety as a drive in accomplishing intellectual tasks—or more precisely about different kinds of anxiety[2]—but the broad picture regarding the value of introversion and neuroticism is reasonably clear. (It is not altogether clear, however, *why* a degree of neuroticism should be an asset in intellectual pursuits.) The introvert will gear himself for sustained application to tasks which involve words, ideas and abstractions; but the extravert will probably attain a more powerful 'drive' in solving concrete problems involving people. He will not be so interested in reducing humanity to a formula; but he may achieve more in dealing with specific and concrete human predicaments. (This book is unlikely to appeal to him.) Unfortunately for him our system of academic assessment does not take his interests and capacities into account.

The present-day university population obtains higher scores on introversion and neuroticism than equally intelligent people who have not been interested in attending a university or who have been denied admission.[3] Even in America, where university entrance is more open to those without strong academic inclinations, university graduates tend to suffer more from serious social-personal maladjustment than those of similar intelligence who have remained outside the university. In Terman's most recent follow-up (1950–5) of his sample of highly gifted (intelligent) Americans, now in their forties, almost twice the proportion of college graduates were found to suffer from 'serious maladjust-

---

[1] See Monica Wilson, *Good Company* (1951).
[2] Cf. D. E. Broadbent, op. cit.: 'there is little doubt that anxiety, in some sense of the word, contributes to rapid conditioning and to good academic achievement. But the exact sense in which this is true is somewhat uncertain. The individual differences may be due to drive or to reactive inhibition: to motivation or to fatigability, if one wishes to keep clear of Hullian terms' (p. 153).
[3] R. Lynn, loc. cit.

ment' compared with those who had not enjoyed a college education.[1]

As a university degree becomes a necessary prerequisite for entry into an ever wider range of occupations, we are preparing for positions of high status a great army of young people who have not necessarily those attributes of personality needed to occupy them effectively—or even very happily. It is perhaps of little consequence that the universities should be staffed predominantly by neurotic introverts. (But if both staff and students score high in these dimensions of personality, the result is unlikely to be a particularly hilarious community. No doubt hilarity is an irrelevant criterion by which to judge the life of a university; but it is doubtful whether work of the highest intellectual originality will be produced where there is no dash of frivolity.)[2] In other institutions this personality type might survive less effectively and perform less useful work.

In the past sustained performance over a narrow range of intellectual skills has not been a general requirement for high office and positions of leadership in English society. In the learned professions this has, quite properly, been required of

[1] Lewis M. Terman and Melita H. Oden, *The Gifted Group in Middle Life. Genetic Studies of Genius* (1959), vol. 5, p. 49. 8·3 per cent of (male) college graduates were 'seriously maladjusted', only 4·6 per cent of those who had not attended college (see Table 10). We urgently need more studies of university students matched with able individuals who did not attend universities. Some American research shows psychological deterioration among students, but no comparison with other populations is made. At Vassar, for example, 'A consistent trend is for seniors to be higher than freshmen on the following scales: Hypochondriasis, Depression, Hysteria, Psychopathic Deviate, Schizophrenia, and Mania.' (See Harold Webster *et al.*, 'Personality Changes in College Students' in Nevitt Sanford (ed.), *The American College* (1962).)

There are indications that American university students are more extraverted and less introverted than English university students, but that they suffer from higher levels of anxiety. Their degree of introversion seems to be similar to that found among English C.A.T. students. See R. B. Cattell and F. W. Warburton, 'A Cross-Cultural Comparison of Patterns of Extraversion and Anxiety', *British Journal of Psychology* (1961), 52.

[2] Since this was written Ferdynand Zweig's depressing book, *The Student in the Age of Anxiety*, has been published. This survey of students at Oxford and Manchester provides further support for the views advanced in this book. Dr Zweig finds the atmosphere of universities heavy and joyless, students anxious, harassed, guilt-ridden (even about their grants), unadventurous and conformist. 'They are not angry young men' (p. xiii), 'there is little doubt that the young are becoming old before their time' (p. xv). 'The students I interviewed did not strike me as young and carefree, on the contrary, they struck me as old, laden with responsibility, care and worry, with nightmares and horror dreams' (p. xiv).

entrants; and since the later nineteenth century, perhaps equally properly, it has been a requirement of the higher civil service. But industry and commerce, social work and public life, and a wide variety of administrative services, have not commonly recruited from the same source. Appointments have been made through influence and patronage, or through proven competence at lower levels of the enterprise. The widespread employment of graduates over a greater range of managerial work is of relatively recent date.

And formerly the graduate was not necessarily, or even perhaps commonly, endowed with the type of personality which alone seems able to secure university entrance, and an adequate degree, today. Indeed, the university man who reached the topmost positions in the nation's life had often, in the eighteenth and nineteenth centuries, failed to take a degree at all.[1] The Colonial Service throughout the twentieth century has been comparatively indifferent to a candidate's performance in academic work and has taken other evidence of capacity into account.[2] Increasingly those who are permitted to pursue higher academic studies have no other capacities which *can* be taken into account.

Any return to methods of selecting the nation's élite which ignored merit as estimated by our institutions of higher education would be offensive to contemporary notions of social justice. If a university degree is to be a necessary qualification for entry into responsible positions in virtually all departments of the nation's life, then men with highly valuable personal qualities—which don't happen to be those which ensure success in academic work —must be admitted to degree courses and helped to make a reasonable showing in the examinations. Much closer supervision of students might be necessary to achieve this. The intelligent individual who is unfortunate enough to be a stable extravert must not be denied the qualifications necessary for entering positions of high responsibility.

But other solutions are infinitely preferable.[3] More diversified

[1] See H. Jenkins and D. C. Jones, 'Social Class of Cambridge University Alumni of the 18th and 19th Centuries', *British Journal of Sociology* (1950), 1. Some 50 per cent of the sons of landowners failed to take a degree but assumed positions of leadership in later life.
[2] See R. Heussler, *Yesterday's Rulers* (1963).
[3] American experience should warn us against over-optimistic expectations that more worthwhile personalities will necessarily result from university education. Extensive

routes into the national élite should be available, in which abilities in other than narrowly defined intellectual exercises are assessed: particularly the skills of human relationship—quiet unruffled confidence in human crises; an outgoing and reassuring approach to colleagues, subordinates and clients; tact and capacity to tolerate uncertain and ambiguous human situations; concern without hypersensitivity; an interest in and concern for actual, concrete individuals, instead of ideas about individuals and formulae which embrace an abstracted aspect of a faceless multitude. Some of our new institutions of higher education must recast their curricula in these terms.

Our society cannot afford to dispense with the services of the intelligent extravert at the highest levels of leadership. Our schools and institutions of higher learning must cater for him and cease to eliminate him along the educational route. If he is more often found in our grammar schools, and following a curriculum which exercises and rewards his special skills (even though these are difficult to assess), we may find a smaller proportion of the young who are accorded high status so resentful and in such apparent conflict as a result of their good fortune.

American research on personality development at the university, while it often presents conflicting results, in general does not offer a re-assuring picture. In particular see the collation of research findings in P. E. Jacob, *Changing Values in College* (New York 1957). For discussions of later research see Nevitt Sanford (ed.), *The American College* (New York 1962). It would be singularly insular and arrogant to assume that we necessarily do better than, say, Vassar and Yale. We do not even bother to do the necessary research into the real consequence of 'educational' experiences. Numerous American inquiries show undergraduates developing somewhat more liberal values (e.g. Plant, 'Changes in Ethnocentricism during College', *Journal of Educational Psychology*, 1958) but declining in general mental health (e.g. Loomis and Green, 'Patterns of Mental Conflict in a Typical State University', *Journal of Abnormal and Social Psychology*, 1947). Deterioration e.g. in 'neurotic trends' has been frankly accepted as a prerequisite of academic education (e.g. Webster, 'Some Quantitative Results', *Journal of Social Issues*, 1956). The rigours of the 'real' world after college may promote a measure of recovery (e.g. Tate and Musick, 'Adjustment Problems of College Students', *Social Forces*, 1954).

B   9

Chapter Two

YOUTH AND SOCIETY

Status: Subjective and Objective

THE hatred with which the mature of Western society
regard the young is a testimony to the latter's importance,
to their power potential and actual. The adolescent has not
enjoyed such economic and social power as is his and hers in
mid-twentieth-century Britain, Europe and America, since the
early days of the classical Industrial Revolution, when rapidly
declining rates of mortality among the young made them worth
taking seriously, and technological change and the reorganization
of industry gave them a strategic position in the nation's economic
life.

Provided they were fortunate enough to escape an apprenticeship, whether 'parish' or otherwise, the young enjoyed status
then as today in the sense of actual social and economic power:
they had a large measure of control over their own lives (for
instance, where they lived and when they married); their parents
were often more dependent on them than they on their parents.
They may not have enjoyed 'accorded status', in the sense
employed by present-day sociologists;[1] then as now they received
only a grudging recognition by their elders of their real social
significance. Today their seniors protect their own position with
a variety of stratagems, planned ostensibly in the best interests
of the young: prolonged tutelage and dependence, exclusion
from adult pursuits, interests and responsibilities, in order to
'protect them from themselves'; extended training schemes of

---

[1] See for example the subjective approach of W. Lloyd Warner and his associates
in the Yankee City studies (*The Social Life of a Modern Community* (1941) etc.), and
J. Hall and C. D. Jones, 'Social Grading of Occupations', *British Journal of Sociology*
(1950), 1. For a very valuable discussion of objective and subjective, Marxist and
anti-Marxist, approaches to status, see S. M. Lipset and R. Bendix, 'Social Status
and Social Structure: A Re-Examination of Data and Interpretations', I and II,
British Journal of Sociology (1951), 2.

negligible educational content which effectively delay the open competition of the young worker with his seniors.

But in spite of the spirited rearguard action which their elders fight, the young achieve power. They have, on a scale without precedent this century, economic power derived from independent earnings; they enter highly skilled occupations; they marry young. It is true that they are without the vote; they receive a bad Press. They are without high status in the sense of enjoying the high regard of others; but they have considerable status (though less than what is potentially theirs) in terms of economic and social independence. It is in this latter, objective, sense, rather than in the subjective sense of rating or appraisal by others, that the term 'status' is employed in this book.

There is evidence (which is supported by inquiries reported below in Chapter Five) that adolescents do not return in equal measure the hostility which adults direct towards them. They are on the whole kindly disposed to their seniors, value their approval and aim to be co-operative with them. On the other hand, they are critical of their coevals and would not ideally meet the full range of their perceived demands and expectations. In general, adults regardless of age and social class consign the young to a self-contained world of juvenile pre-occupations; they strongly resist the notion that in their late teens they might qualify for entry into adult pursuits and rights: they resent their 'precociousness', their tendency to earlier marriage and to higher earnings; they reject the idea that perhaps the young might end their legal minority before the age of twenty-one, enter into full citizenship and exercise the vote.

When, in 1963, the author attempted to discover the attitude of adults towards the earlier entry of adolescents into adult life, he found an overwhelming rejection of the idea, but a general agreement that adolescents should inhabit a segregated, and virtually autonomous, non-adult social sphere. A random sample of adults, taken from the electoral roll of a city in the north Midlands, were sent by post a questionnaire which asked for their degree of agreement or disagreement with four propositions: two related to the segregation of adolescents from the world of their seniors, two to their possible earlier entry into it. The former propositions read: 'Adolescents should be encouraged to develop their own distinctive way of living, e.g. in dress, leisure pursuits, musical tastes etc.' and 'Adolescents are entitled to their fun, even if it is not altogether to our taste'. The latter propositions were: 'Young people of 17 or 18 are quite fit to have the vote' and 'Teenage marriage is more generally desirable'. A response to each statement was asked for on a 5-point scale: 'Strongly agree', 'Agree', 'Uncertain', 'Disagree', 'Strongly Disagree'.

The questionnaires were sent to 200 adults: sixty-one (30 per cent) were returned completed as requested. The returns were biased towards the higher occupational groups.[1] Equal numbers of men and women completed the questionnaires.

In order to analyse the returns respondents were divided into 'Upper Class' (Registrar-General's occupational grades I, II, and IIIA—routine non-manual) and 'Lower Class' (occupational grades IIIB—skilled manual, IV and V). Married women were assigned to a 'social class' according to their husbands' occupations. Seventy-three-point-eight per cent of the sample were 'Upper Class', 26·2 per cent 'Lower Class'.

There were no significant differences according to 'social class', age or sex in the responses to these four statements. There was an overwhelming rejection of teenage marriage and an earlier right to vote, and a correspondingly great acceptance of the autonomous life of the young.

TABLE I

ADULTS' ATTITUDES TO THE SEGREGATION AND INTEGRATION
OF YOUTH

	Strongly agree and Agree	Uncertain	Strongly disagree and Disagree
'*Vote at 17 or 18*' and '*Teenage marriage generally desirable*' (Combined N: 122)	14·7% (N 18)	12·4% (N 15)	72·9% (N 89)
'*Entitled to their fun*' and '*Distinctive way of life*' (Combined N: 122)	80·4% (N 98)	4·9% (N 6)	14·7% (N 18)

[1] Eighteen per cent of the city's male population were in the Registrar-General's occupational grades I and II, 50 per cent of the respondents were in these grades.

The adults in this inquiry were as much in favour of the young living their own separate life as they were against their earlier assumption of adult roles. Both attitudes may, perhaps, be regarded as in some sense 'favourable' to the young: the objection to early marriage and the right to vote might well be justified as an attempt to protect them against themselves. But however laudable the motive might be, the intention is to define a separate population, insulated from the world of the mature. It may be that this population is truly immature; what is astonishing is the extent to which, in spite of such attitudes, it is not.

Making Adolescents

The adolescent as a distinct species is the creation of modern social attitudes and institutions. A creature neither child nor adult, he is a comparatively recent socio-psychological invention, scarcely two centuries old. Distinctive social institutions have been fashioned to accommodate him; psychologically he has been made more or less to fit them, moulded by appropriate rewards and penalties.

He is discouraged from learning many adult roles, but may be required to learn others, such as the role of wage-earner; but 'the remainder of his roles may not be so very different from those he learned in childhood'.[1] Personality traits which 'worked' in childhood may still secure satisfactions and approval in adolescence and so be perpetuated: 'social lines of facilitation'[2] are kept open and juvenile behaviour persists beyond its natural or necessary term. The psychologists are pleased to report the continuity of childhood and adolescent personality.[3]

But what is even more striking, in the few studies that have been made, is the continuity of adolescent and adult personality. Symonds's intensive though small-scale follow-up study of a group of New York adolescents over a period of 13 years (from 1940 to 1953) led him to the view that 'the concept of adoles-

[1] Hans Gerth and C. Wright Mills, *Character and Social Structure* (London 1954), p. 157.
[2] Ibid., p. 159.
[3] See C. M. Fleming, *Adolescence* (1948): 'the development of the young human being is both more continuous, more complex and more highly differentiated than the psychologists of the past and the popular writers of today would lead us to suppose' (p. 42).

cence as a separate period of life with distinctive characteristics recedes . . .'[1]

Interviews and a Picture-Story Test were the main instruments used for exploring deeper levels of the personality in 1940; in 1953 (when the subjects were aged from 26 to 31, had often in the meantime been engaged in military service, had in some cases enjoyed a university education, and were now established in their careers and founding families of their own), the Rorsharch test was the principal method of investigation. Physical characteristics had persisted over thirteen years, and so had readily observable patterns of behaviour: hobbies, nervous signs, aggressiveness in response to interviews and tests. Anxious adult personalities were foreshadowed in the anxieties shown in adolescent fantasies; ineffective adults had shown a deep sense of inferiority thirteen years before. What they had been at 13, they were, in essence, at 30.

It is true that there were some changes in the themes which pre-occupied subjects in the earlier and the later tests: the changes were not always towards greater 'maturity'. Whilst there was a decrease in themes of violent aggression, there was an increase in themes of depression and in wishful thinking. But the most remarkable fact was the comparative lack of change, which must throw grave doubts on any attempt to delineate a specific 'adolescent personality'. 'One of the outstanding findings of this study is the remarkable persistence of personality trends over the thirteen-year period. Growing out of adolescence does not mean giving up certain personality trends and taking on others, but rather meeting life's experiences with the same personality equipment one has been provided with from earlier years.'[2] (There is little hope for the adolescent in all this that he will 'grow out of it', even if profound experiences intervene. Higher education may be extravagant in its claims to effect, even through the most costly residential and tutorial systems, any profound modification of the personality already established in the earlier teens. It is worth trying to find out what returns we *can* reasonably expect, in terms of personality development, from an ever greater provision of higher education.)

In their moral values as well as their personality traits young

[1] Percival M. Symonds, *From Adolescent to Adult* (1961), p. 194.
[2] Ibid., pp. 195–6.

American adolescents have been shown to differ little from mature adults. A representative sample of thirty-four out of 'Prairie City's' 120 adolescents who were born in 1933 were intensively studied by Peck, Havighurst and their colleagues between 1943 and 1950. Sociometric tests showed that, in general, those children enjoyed the highest reputation who were perceived to have the type of moral character of which mature and intelligent adults (the research staff) approved. 'In the main, even with the inclusion of the discrepant cases, this adolescent group proved to like and to admire its members in terms of the same sociomoral characteristics which the conference staff defined as central to good moral character.'[1]

Indeed, Peck and Havighurst make no distinction between 'adult' and 'adolescent' phases of character development. Five 'ideal types' of character are postulated for different stages of development: Amoral (Infancy), Expedient (Early Childhood), Conforming or Irrational-Conscientious (Later Childhood), and Rational-Altruistic (Adulthood *and* Adolescence). In their studies of Prairie City's adolescents Peck and Havighurst found individuals who approximated to all five character-types: only a quarter of their sample approximated to the model of maturity. But they estimate that 'a sizeable minority' of the adult American population is still at the Amoral or Expedient stage, and 'perhaps over 50 per cent' Conforming or Irrational-Conscientious.[2] No greater proportion of the nation's adults than of their sample of 16-year-olds was thought to be mature (Rational-Altruistic). The 'maturity' of the adolescent subjects, like the maturity of adults, does not mean finality of development, with no room for increase in wisdom, judgement, knowledge, insight and understanding. But in their values and attitudes and capacity for altruism and rational discrimination in their personal relationships, a representative sample of 16-year-olds seems unlikely to be inferior to a representative sample of the adult population.

[1] See R. F. Peck and R. J. Havighurst, *The Psychology of Character Development* (New York 1960), p. 139. 'This is not to say that adolescents are completely mature, accurate judges of the most important values, or of the morally best or worst in individuals, in all cases . . . On the whole, though, the adolescent *group's* judgement is sound, much more often than not, when compared with mature standards of conduct and moral values' (p. 129). Of course, all the adolescents of a community are being compared with a highly selected group of highly educated research workers.
[2] Ibid., p. 197.

Youth and Society

Adolescents whose overt behaviour is suitably non-adult can, however, be made. They can be excluded from responsible participation in affairs, rewarded for dependency, penalized for inconvenient displays of initiative, and so rendered sufficiently irresponsible to confirm the prevailing teenager-stereotype. They can be made into ineffectual outsiders.

This is more difficult if some adult roles have been encouraged even before adolescence—which is often the case with girls, perhaps particularly first-born girls.[1] In adolescence they may be required to unlearn adult behaviour and attitudes, which were previously approved, as a prelude to becoming 'truly adult'. The pre-pubescent girl may have years of training in 'helping around the house' and assuming considerable responsibility in family life; when she shows the same independence and initiative in adolescence, now perhaps over a more extended field, her behaviour is lamented as 'forward', 'sophisticated', 'precocious'. Boys do not run the same risk: there are no adult roles which they can begin assuming, with their elders' approval, in childhood. For them pre-pubescent years provide a suitable preparation in irresponsibility for the role of adolescent.

The girl who was not, in fact, 'brought on' in childhood, will have her dependency deepened and confirmed in adolescence. Longitudinal studies of twenty-seven American males and twenty-seven females born between 1930 and 1939 showed remarkable stability in the dependent behaviour of females from infancy to adulthood. Not one whose dependency rating was high as a child secured a low dependency rating as an adult. With the males there was far more change. Twenty per cent were rated very dependent as children, very independent as adults.[2] Not only are adolescents made, but also adults. While dependency in girls may continue to secure reward and gratification into adult life, the males, as young adults, are given every inducement by parents and peers to unlearn the dependency which was formerly approved and to show the independence thought fitting to their new age and status.

Whatever the potential of the adolescent, his actual perform-

[1] See E. E. Sampson, 'Birth Order, Need Achievement, and Conformity', *Journal of Abnormal and Social Psychology* (1962), 64.
[2] J. Kagan and H. A. Moss, 'The Stability of Passive and Dependent Behaviour from Childhood through Adulthood', *Child Development* (1960), 31.

16

ance is likely to be reasonably close to what adult society rewards most and penalizes least. He is what society makes him. He can be 'explained' only partly in terms of individual psychology: historical and sociological data must complement the psychological to account for his behaviour: 'En effet, il n'est plus possible d'observer les jeunes seulement dans le cadre de la psychologie. On ne peut se satisfaire de la seule description ou analyse des traits et des réactions qui caractérisent individuellement chacun d'entre eux. Il faut encore observer les phénomènes historiques et sociologiques qui, dans une grande mesure, déterminent ces traits et ces réactions'.[1]

The Realism of Youth

The social institutions of contemporary Britain—particularly our educational institutions—have fashioned adolescents characterized by a degree of realism commonly supposed to be the very hallmark of the mature adult. Many investigators have been both surprised and dismayed by the down-to-earth and practical appraisal which the young in post-war Britain make of their present condition and future prospects. They accurately perceive the implications for their future lives and careers of the educational provision which they receive after the age of eleven. They neither expect nor even desire jobs which are out of line with the level of their educational competence; in their early teens they expect to marry at the age which is in fact most common among the workers they expect to join; the majority of them know with a remarkable degree of accuracy what they will earn in the jobs they expect, both initially and in adult years.

These generalizations are based on a survey of schoolchildren's aspirations which the author directed in junior, modern, and grammar schools in the Midlands in 1961;[2] they are supported by other work reported by Jahoda[3] and Veness.[4] The latter's inquiry (1956) among 1,300 boys and girls aged 15 to 18 in modern, grammar, and technical schools showed how

[1] Jean Jousselin, *Jeunesse Fait Social Méconnu* (1959), p. 7.
[2] For a report of this survey see W. Liversidge, 'Life Chances', *The Sociological Review* (1962), 10.
[3] Gustav Jahoda, 'Social Class Attitudes and Levels of Occupational Aspiration in Secondary Modern School Leavers', *British Journal of Psychology* (1953), 44.
[4] Thelma Veness, *School Leavers: Their Aspirations and Expectations* (1962).

realistic were the ambitions of young people when they looked forward to their future careers: their aims were sensible, responsible, ordinary. Jahoda's more limited investigation (1949–50) of the aspirations of school-leavers from four secondary modern schools in a Lancashire town showed how even in fantasy these young people had no desire to rise to the top of the social hierarchy; and, when they expressed realistic desires, while there was a general appreciation of the job 'with good prospects', preferences were closely in accord with the possibilities of their world.

In the inquiry in schools in the Midlands (1961) in which 616 children were involved, similar attitudes were found. The realistic job-expectations (as opposed to the 'fantasy choices') of modern-school boys in their final year were, not surprisingly, more modest than those of senior grammar-school boys; but even their fantasy choices did not soar away from their immediate world and possibilities. 'Indeed the fantasy choices of these boys are at a distressingly mundane and realistic level; the majority rarely leave their immediate world. We had expected that in their flights of fancy they would select the more exciting occupations such as pilot, professional footballer, explorer, "pop" singer, or even the old-fashioned engine-driver. Instead, we have the boy who expects to be a labourer at the brick-yard choosing the very same job in fantasy, and the potential rubber moulder who, when offered the whole world from which to choose, still wants to be a rubber moulder.'

The subjects of this study were also asked to state what they thought they would earn when they started in the job they expected, and what they thought they'd be earning at the age of 30. Their estimates were compared with the rates actually prevailing in the various occupations and accorded closely with them. Modern-school boys tended slightly to overestimate what they would be earning at the age of 30, but their forecasts were more modest the lower the ability-stream: A- and B-stream boys expected a median wage of £17 a week, C-stream boys £14 13s, and D-stream boys £12. Even the ages at which they expected to marry were closely in line with prevailing trends. The modern-school boys expected to marry at a median age of 22·7 years: the median age at marriage of males in the region who married before they were 35 (93 per cent of all marriages) was 23·1 years. The ages for girls were 20·9 years and 21·2 years respectively. 'The general picture that emerges from this study is one of startlingly accurate appraisal of life chances by children, and a shrewd appreciation of the social and economic implications of their placing within the educational system . . . Having accepted the role they are to play in life they rarely venture out of it even in fantasy.'

The Conservatism of the Young

There is no immediate prospect of any massive rebellion by the young against their condition and the dominant customs, trends and institutions of our society. Never (at least since the later eighteenth century) have they given such support as they do today to the institution of marriage; perhaps, too, they were never so satisfied with the economic order and the jobs it offers them. Job-satisfaction among young graduates is perhaps not surprising: a recent survey carried out by the University of Nottingham into the careers and attitudes of 614 men and women who graduated there between 1950 and 1958 concluded that: 'On the whole, graduates seem content with the quality and purpose of the job in which they are engaged; most considered their work to be of benefit both to themselves and to the community, although a sizeable fraction are only moderately convinced of this. Only three graduates from the sample thought that their current work was of use neither to themselves nor to the community . . .'[1] Yet these graduates had not, in the main, moved into the higher and more prestige-bearing professions (no less than 42 per cent of them were teaching[2]). Modest aspirations had been satisfactorily matched with modest preferment.

Post-war studies among more representative groups of young workers have revealed similar high levels of job-satisfaction. In a national sample of 1,400 males and 450 females aged 15 to 19, 77 per cent of the former claimed that they were 'very satisfied' with their present jobs, and no less than 83 per cent of the latter.

[1] See University of Nottingham: *Convocation Newsletter* (1962), 3.
[2] Teachers seem to enjoy a higher measure of job-satisfaction than is commonly supposed: see W. G. A. Rudd and S. Wiseman, 'Sources of Dissatisfaction among a Group of Teachers', *British Journal of Educational Psychology* (1962), 32.

Only 5 per cent of the men and 2 per cent of the women were 'not satisfied'.[1] There was a tendency for males whose first job was unskilled to have been less satisfied with it than other categories of worker (only 38 per cent had been 'very satisfied', compared with 67 per cent—the highest proportion in any occupational group—and of agricultural workers).

Those who actively challenge the established social order, its values, institutions and policies, are a small minority of the young: juvenile delinquents at (in the main) lower social levels, 'Beats' and C.N.D.[2] supporters at (in the main) higher levels. Delinquency statistics are notoriously difficult to interpret; but in the peak age-group (14 years since 1948, 13 years before) only 2·7 per cent were convicted of indictable offences.[3] (If children from white-collar homes invariably received official penalties like the rest, the figure would no doubt be somewhat higher.) Those *cautioned* by the police for indictable offences account for another 0·6 per cent of the 14-year-olds; and convictions for non-indictable offences (such as drunkenness and disorderly behaviour) account for a further 0·4 per cent of young men aged 17–21 (the peak period for offences in this category).[4] Disturbing though these figures are, they indicate criminal deviation in less than 4 per cent of the age-group most at risk.

There is no doubt that the proportion of convictions has risen steeply since 1938; there is little doubt that it will continue to rise; for at the very base of contemporary society there exists a population of young persons who are exceptional in finding the present social order quite unrewarding, are likely to find it ever less rewarding, and will be prone, in consequence, to seek status in their own circle in terms at variance with prevailing values.[5] These are the less successful children in the secondary-modern schools; they cannot blame, as their grandfathers with justification

[1] Leslie T. Wilkins, *The Adolescent in Britain* (1955), p. 59.
[2] 3,000 on the Aldermaston March 1958, 15,000 by 1962—less than a quarter of a good football match attendance. Probably only a minority are teenagers: see survey in Welwyn Garden City reported in *The Guardian* (25 May 1963), p. 3.
[3] See The Albermarle Report: *The Youth Service in England and Wales* (1960), Appendix 9.
[4] See *Criminal Statistics England and Wales 1961* (1962), Appendices IIIA and IIIB.
[5] Cf. M. Cohen, *Delinquent Boys* (1956). 'Certain children are denied status in the respectable society because they cannot meet the criteria of the respectable status system. The delinquent subculture deals with these problems by providing criteria of status which these children *can* meet.'

were able to do, the injustices of the social system for their present position and future prospects. They are bereft of the excuse which might salvage their self-esteem; they can blame nothing but their own incapacity. For them we are fashioning an intolerable social order.

It is this population which is likely to find it ever harder to find employment, for the proportion of unskilled jobs in the economy is diminishing. Mays has underlined their predicament in his study of Liverpool's down-town schools: 'it looks very much as though the majority of the children who leave the Crown Street schools are going to fill the unskilled manual jobs which carry the lowest social prestige . . . It is more than doubtful whether or not there will be enough jobs of this sort to absorb all the young men and boys of the central city areas. The demand for unskilled manual workers is likely to lessen rather than increase during the next twenty years or so, and if that occurs, there is going to be a high proportion of unemployment.'[1] It is doubly unfortunate that those who are likely to face these frustrations are precisely those least well-equipped to respond creatively, with imaginative plans for remedial social change. Their response is more likely to be, at the best, apathetic, at the worst, negative and destructive.

But the broad picture of contemporary youth is not of a population either actually or potentially deviant—or even particularly adventurous. At the university level young men self-consciously groom themselves to fit into the organizational life of our public services, research stations, commerce and industry. The leadership they will exercise is, in Weber's term, 'rational-legal'—with only the rarest touch of charisma. We cannot hope to produce a great army of graduates remarkable for their charismatic qualities; but our own universities in the past—and those of Europe and Asia even more so—have been more remarkable for the social and political challenge their students have made.[2] Our modern undergraduates, as Michael Young has recently observed, are in danger of 'becoming cautious old men at 20'.[3] The student population of our mid-

[1] J. B. Mays, *Education and the Urban Child* (1962), p. 157.
[2] For the significance of university students in the Revolutions of 1848 in the Habsburg Empire, particularly in Vienna and Prague, see A. J. P. Taylor, *The Habsburg Monarchy 1809–1918* (1948) pp. 58–9.
[3] See 'The Case for a National University', *The Observer* (22 September 1963), p. 10.

twentieth century universities constitutes a negligible political force. Its servility ensures modest and comfortable—though not generally extravagant—social and economic rewards.

So security-minded are the young of mid-twentieth century Britain that their attitudes and behaviour have been lamented as contrary to 'nature': the assumption being that the mere process of growth, regardless of the social context in which it occurs, automatically brings a period of questioning established ways and experimenting in new forms of social experience.

Logan and Golberg were disturbed to find, in 1950, so high a proportion of the 18-year-old men whom they investigated in a London borough so set in their jobs—and already looking forward to the pensions which would eventually accrue: 'It can be questioned whether the absence of labour turnover at this age, whose hallmark is usually considered to be curiosity and experiment, is a healthy sign.'[1] These young men were a cross-section of the population, representing all social levels, engaged in or preparing for occupations ranging from labouring to professional work. It was the labourers who were most restive; but in general, neither in the attitudes of these young men to work or society, were they other than tamely conformist.

Logan and Goldberg observe that 'The lack of creative or constructive leisure pursuits of these lads is striking . . .' 'Although late adolescence and early adulthood are usually considered to be phases of adventure and experiment, these weekend and holiday programmes show a conspicuous absence of such characteristics.' They were not interested in the life of the community or the management of its affairs; they had little political interest. 'They convey the impression of passive acceptance of the world around them. This picture vividly contrasts with the prevalent notion of restless youth eager to explore and experiment . . .'

These young men were growing up during World War II; and just as post-war delinquency is frequently attributed to a war-time background, so may this less striking and disruptive form of 'unnatural' behaviour. But both delinquency and passive conformity in the young are more economically explicable in terms of the contemporary social scene, in which they are actually found. The social and economic rewards which the majority of

[1] See 'Rising Eighteen in a London Suburb', *British Journal of Sociology* (1953), 4.

the post-war young enjoy are sufficient to account for their docility, the exclusiveness of adults' pursuits sufficient to account for their inactivity. What *is* there for them to do as they wait in limbo? They can only wait around until they are allowed to be adult: to marry, make homes, and have a responsible interest in community affairs. On the other hand, the social disabilities of the least gifted minority are sufficient to account for their less acceptable but more vigorous forms of protest.

Education as Ritual

The more highly rewarded young are expected to pay a price: they realize this, and for the most part enter into a tacit bargain with their seniors who exact it. The price is deferred social gratification in return for augmented gratification in the end: the deferment takes the form of industrial apprenticeships which the apprentices themselves may regard, after the first few months, as futile; or extended education in formal institutions which may have little relevance to life present or future. The more perceptive young recognize that this is a game devised by their elders in which they will be wise to co-operate.

A realistic re-appraisal of the social and economic role of apprenticeship in our contemporary society is long overdue. The history of apprenticeship has been idealized;[1] its value to the young, as well as to industry, is today taken as axiomatic. But as we have seen in the recent economic history of the North-East of England (1962–3), extended schemes of apprenticeship may be advocated not because industry is starved of trained manpower, but because it has a surplus: apprenticeship is a means of mopping up, at least temporarily, reservoirs of otherwise unwanted juvenile labour. The proposals (1963) of Lord Hailsham, as Minister with special responsibilities for the North-East, that more skilled

[1] Apprenticeship is long overdue for historical re-appraisal. Extravagant claims have been made for its educational value in the past which are contrary to the weight of evidence. 'In its best days apprenticeship was not only a system of technical instruction, it was also a method of education, and indeed the only method available for the majority of boys': O. J. Dunlop and R. D. Denman, *English Apprenticeship* (1912). See also G. M. Trevelyan, *English Social History* (1946), pp. 192 and 321 for similar complimentary judgements. The history of apprenticeship—even for such skilled occupations as chemist—is in fact a dismal story of futility and exploitation. See for example William Lucas, *A Quaker Journal*, vol. I, p. 44 for an account of an apprenticeship to a chemist (premium £250) in the early nineteenth century.

manpower should be trained at a time when the building industry was counting unemployed craftsmen in thousands, did not commend itself to the unions.[1] Apprenticeship has traditionally served as a means of regulating entry into trades and protecting established workmen from the competition of junior entrants. The content of apprenticeship training has often borne little relationship to the actual requirements of the job. There are areas of industry which urgently require the enhanced skills which apprenticeship can provide (perhaps particularly 'human relations skills' at middle and lower levels of management, as the North-east Trading Council has discovered); but a careful distinction needs to be drawn between apprenticeship which enables and apprenticeship which disables. (Often what is wanted is not more apprenticeships but more jobs.) The former may serve the interests of the young as well as the economy; the latter the interests of an entrenched gerontocracy.

More extended education has been justified on the grounds that for adult life in our 'complex society' a more and more protracted preparation is necessary. But formal education may be, as Cobbett trenchantly observed in his *Advice to Young Men*, a means of disabling people for life. It may seriously retard the capacity to make mature decisions and adjustments. 'If boys live only with boys,' maintained Cobbett, 'their ideas will continue to be boyish; if they see and hear and converse with nobody but boys, how are they to have the thoughts and characters of men?' Extended school education was a serious handicap which no careful and considerate parent would wish to inflict on a child: 'to confine (boys) to the society of boys, is to retard their arrival at years of discretion; and in case of adverse circumstances in a pecuniary way, where, in all creation, is there so helpless a mortal as a boy who has been always at school?'

Cobbett's observations may have been justified in view of the type of schooling available in his day;[2] since then the schoolboy

[1] See Bernard Ingham on the training of youth, *The Guardian*, 25 September 1963, p. 7.
[2] Similar doubts have assailed at least one modern parent: 'During a recent discussion on 'A' levels, university grants, &c. (a favourite topic among parents of sixth formers these days) I was a little shocked to hear a fellow guest say that they had had no worries whatsoever with their children. "You see," she said, "they are all semi-morons and simply loathed the thought of more studies and university life. They have all found themselves remunerative jobs and are now completely independent. Aren't we lucky?" "Are they lucky?" I asked my husband on the way

world has been more thoroughly interpenetrated by adult counsellors and guides. But even today observers have noted a greater tendency to immaturity among those (more able) pupils who are destined to remain longest at school. Hoggart has suggested that even their sexual growth appears to be delayed[1] and that the immaturity of the grammar-school girl of 14 or 15 stands in striking contrast to the development of secondary modern-school girls of the same age. (The Kinsey evidence indicates that heterosexual activity is likely to be longer delayed the higher the educational level of the American male, but substitute sexual activities, perhaps promoting stronger feelings of guilt, may be more common.)

There is strong evidence, which is reported below in Chapter Six, that the grammar schools promote in their pupils conflicts and frustrations which do not beset the children in secondary modern schools, who are nearer to adult life. It is probable that they are taught by teachers who are more aloof, and are actively discouraged from becoming involved in the life of their neighbourhoods (which may be 'lowering'). Their immaturity is educationally induced. Their outlook on life, on their friends, on the world and on school is more negative and despondent than the outlook of their contemporaries in the modern school.

The argument from the supposed 'complexity' of the modern world is a subterfuge—or at best a rationalization—for keeping in prolonged dependence and immaturity those who will eventually be well rewarded for their self-discipline. Hollingshead, commenting on the sociological implications of the rise of the

[1] See R. Hoggart, *The Uses of Literacy* (Pelican Books 1962), pp. 298 and 365.

home. We reviewed our own situation. Our son, having spent four years at Oxbridge (on a partial grant) and gained a second class honours degree in science (with which we were delighted), declares he hasn't a scientific brain and wishes to study law and become a barrister. This means another three years as an impecunious student. Our daughter, after leaving public school at 18, spent a year at a residential secretarial college on the south coast. After several jobs she has now become bored with an office stool and has taken a job with a travel agent (pocket money only). She spends winters in Switzerland and summers in Greece or Spain, "resting" at home between whiles. Has our skimping, i.e. doing without good holidays, meals in restaurants, adequate help in the house and garden, been in vain? Would we spend so large a portion of our income on education again? A difficult question to answer at this stage, but I think it will be "Yes".' (A Correspondent in *The Times*, 23 September 1963, p. 13.)

American high school, expresses similar doubts about the reasons usually advanced for requiring more prolonged education into middle and late adolescence: 'Although this movement (to establish high schools) developed under the guise of the need for more training for adult life, the training given has been largely limited to intellectual pursuits; practically, it has extended the period of dependency on the family for four or five years in the "middle classes", and increasingly in the working class.'[1]

Our urban, industrial and technical society has been contrasted with non-literate societies in its requirement of ever longer formal education to maintain and develop its techniques and institutions. It is possible that our Western society requires a more thoughtful social preparation of the young; but this is precisely what the schools have, in general, failed to give. They have continued to place their major emphasis on the transmission of knowledge. And yet it is in just this respect that the educational institutions of a literate society can afford to be more cavalier than the training system of a non-literate people. Education in the sense of factual instruction and the memorizing of information is less necessary for the former than for the latter: if a generation of a primitive society fails to do its homework, the knowledge is irrecoverably lost. Their technicians cannot look up the formula (or more properly, perhaps, the incantation) which they have collectively forgotten, in the back of this year's engineers' diary.

'Civilization' makes the major content of our traditional education less necessary and not more. If we look closely at the learning which is required by the young of a 'primitive' society, the scope of the 'syllabus' may make our G.C.E. or even degree requirements seem puny. Thus the girls' initiation ceremonies among the Bemba of Northern Rhodesia, described by Audrey Richards,[2] call for a formidable knowledge of traditional rhymes, incantations and rites by both novices and initiates.

[1] A. B. Hollingshead, *Elmtown's Youth* (1949), p. 150. Cf. J. K. Galbraith, *The Affluent Society* (Pelican Books 1962): 'We have excluded youngsters from the labour market, partly on the ground that labour at too early an age is unduly painful and injurious to health, and partly to make way for educational opportunity. But while we have felt it possible to dispense with the goods that the youngsters produce, we have yet to provide them, at least in full and satisfactory measure, with the education that their exemption from labour was designed to make possible' (p. 272).
[2] Audrey Richards, *Chisungu* (1954).

Margaret Read has described the learning required of a young Ngoni tribesman growing up to manhood:[1] the reckoning of time and of the seasons; cosmology and the interpretation of the heavens; tribal history and customary law; veterinary knowledge and skills in the care of cattle; hunting techniques and the skills of building and other manual crafts. The girls undertook an elaborate training in the preparation of food, the arts of household management, bead- and leather-work, the arts of speech, dancing and deportment. Formerly men married in their late twenties: it was only with the advent of an allegedly more complex Western civilization and opportunities for employment in Western enterprises, that this prolonged preparation for adult life became unnecessary and the usual age at which men and women married steeply declined.

Life in a 'civilized' society is in many ways simpler and easier to learn than life in a non-literate tribe. The structure of the language may well be simpler; social forms and institutions less elaborate; areas of knowledge and understanding which are considered essential qualifications for adult life in the 'simpler' societies of little or no importance. The kinship system is a comparatively light burden on the growing child's understanding and memory: he has a more limited range of behaviour and attitudes to learn towards different kinsmen. Though he may require some understanding of machines, he can get by—and usually does—with a negligible understanding of animal behaviour, psychology and anatomy; in our secular society he will be accorded adult status without proven competence in the orthodox theology (although a detailed knowledge of the organization and events of contemporary sports may be virtually obligatory). He lives in a society which, though far more populous, may have a much simpler social hierarchy than those of many African and Oceanic tribesfolk.

On the other hand, he will be confronted by a wider range of conflicting institutions and beliefs, between which he may have to choose—and Margaret Mead has argued that Western societies must educate primarily to enable people to make choices with wisdom and in the light of adequate information. And it is doubtless true that for a minority of men and women who are entering the scientific and traditional learned professions ever

[1] Margaret Read, *Children of their Fathers* (1959).

longer education is necessary if they are to understand an expanding body of knowledge, techniques and ideas. What is doubtful is whether a more extended intellectual training for the majority of our young people is justified either in terms of a 'more complex social order' or even in terms of the personal fulfilment which, it is too confidently assumed, should result. Whatever personal fulfilment should theoretically accrue is likely to be offset by the self-disparagement which exclusion from the world of vital and important issues—the world of adults—will in all likelihood promote.

If more of our youth are to be schooled ever longer (and for political reasons this is increasingly probable), it is vital that more serious consideration be given to the social experiences that are provided within the framework of formal education. It is not sufficient, for the majority, that they should be subjected to a prolonged ritual the significance of which they can barely grasp. The grammar schools have evolved an elaborate ritual: as Dent has argued, 'The grammar school was never a "second stage"; it was a highly specialized form of education . . . more and more a ritual, a kind of prolonged initiation ordeal necessary for the acquirement of indication of superior social status'.[1] Whatever validity this ordeal may have for a small élite, it has none for the rank and file.

Orientations of the Young

In England the tripartite system of secondary education has superseded family, friends and social class as the frame of reference from which the young take their bearings for their future lives and careers. It seems likely that where the educational system, perhaps in the name of democracy, refuses to provide this service for young adolescents, more informal social institutions will do so: the influence of social class and of friendship groupings will be enhanced. Thus the peer group must do for American youth what educational selection and segregation do for the young in England—provide them with associates with similar aspirations from whom they can learn behaviour appropriate to their social and occupational goals.

There are strong indications that in an educational system—or

[1] H. C. Dent, *Secondary Education for All* (1949), pp. 1-2.

within a single school—which segregates ability groups and, at least by implication, through differentiated curricula, prepares them for different levels of occupation and social standing, friendship groups do not form along social class lines. Socio-metric studies with grammar-school boys have failed to show self-segregation according to social background;[1] in streamed junior schools friendships have been found to be 'random' with respect to social origins.[2] But in unstreamed junior schools, the social extremes tend to be self-choosing; boys of intermediate social standing may find friends at either extreme, but the inter-mediate girls, like those of highest and lowest social rank, tend also to be inbred, choosing one another.[3] When schools refuse to establish distinctions, children must.

In sharp contrast with the position which appears to prevail in English grammar schools is the self-segregation by social class which has been widely reported in studies of the 'democratic' American high school. Thus Hollingshead found in a mid-western town's high school that the type of curriculum for which children opted was closely related to their social position: 64 per cent of the children in social classes I and II entered on the (academic) College Preparatory course, none of them entered on the Commercial course; but only 4 per cent of the children in social class V (the lowest) entered the former course, but 38 per cent entered the latter.[4]

Even more striking was the self-preference within the different social class groups in the children's choice of friends. The girls at every level gave more than 70 per cent of their 'best friend' choices at their own social level; there was a similar intensity of self-preference among the boys except in social class V: 63 per cent of the boys in this class gave their choices to other class-V boys.[5] In short, social-class background was closely associated with all those school activities which were likely to determine future career and life-style: with the curriculum followed, with

[1] A. N. Oppenheim, 'Social Status and Clique Formation among Grammar School Boys', *British Journal of Sociology* (1958), 4.
[2] See W. A. L. Blyth, 'Sociometry, Prefects and Peaceful Co-Existence in a Junior School', *Sociological Review* (1958), 6.
[3] See J. C. Willig, *Social Implications of Streaming in the Junior School* (1961), unpublished M.Ed. thesis, University of Leicester.
[4] A. B. Hollingshead, op. cit., Table X, p. 462.
[5] Ibid., Table 12, p. 216.

involvement in school societies, with friendships formed, and with age of leaving. (All Elmtown's class-I adolescents between the ages of 13 and 19 were still at school; only 11·3 per cent of the class-V adolescents.)

The American adolescent of humble origins who has the ability and the desire to be socially mobile (to 'better himself'), will not find an educational institution designed especially for him; but he may find a high status peer group to which he can attach himself and from which he can learn the attitudes and behaviour which will assist him. Talcot Parsons and Winston White have examined the way in which the peer group assumes the role which the educational system declines: 'Broadly, then, we suggest that the individual headed for higher occupational status will choose peer groups that tend on the whole to facilitate his progress in this direction'.[1]

The American peer group has the job which in England is undertaken by the system of educational selection and segregation. The English peer group is consequently of less importance and, within a particular type of school, can afford to be 'democratic' in its membership. The peer group stands behind the American high school, testing out the individual's fitness for ascent. Selection by the peer group occurs in the absence of selection by the school authorities. 'The schools . . . cannot serve as mediating integrating mechanisms except so far as types of schools themselves are differentiated'.[2] And it is the pride of American democracy that types of school are not differentiated.

In England a boy's outlook and future prospects tend to be determined by the type of school he attends; in America they tend to be determined by his family background and the friends he makes. Youmans set out to test the hypothesis that 'Position in the social structure, that is, social origin, is more important in formulating the occupational expectations of youth than are such factors as the home, the school, work experience and type of community'.[3] His research in the schools of Michigan amply supported this contention. There was a strong tendency for

[1] Talcott Parsons and Winston White, 'The Link between Character and Society' in S. M. Lipset and Leo Lowenthal (eds.), *Culture and Social Character* (1961), p. 127.
[2] Talcott Parsons and Winston White, loc. cit., p. 128.
[3] E. G. Youmans, 'Occupational Expectations of Twelfth Grade Michigan Boys', *Journal of Experimental Education* (1956), 24.

boys to expect jobs at the same occupational level as their fathers. 'The occupational expectations of the boys substantially and significantly reflect their position in the social structure . . .'

In England this is not the case; the type of school attended is more important than 'social class' in determining levels of occupational aspiration. In the Midland survey of school-children's aspirations to which reference has already been made, senior scholars in grammar schools had very high occupational aspirations whatever their social origins; but in modern schools 'upper class'[1] boys had far less frequently real expectations of 'upper class' employment. The expectations of upper class girls in modern schools were also depressed, but to a less marked extent. The following table[2] gives the occupational expectations of senior boys and girls in the two types of school:

TABLE II

OCCUPATIONAL EXPECTATIONS IN GRAMMAR AND MODERN SCHOOLS

Subjects	Grammar Schools		Modern Schools	
	Upper Class Choice %	Lower Class Choice %	Upper Class Choice %	Lower Class Choice %
	Boys			
	N 44		N 172	
Upper Class	93·1	6·9	43·0	57·0
Lower Class	93·3	6·7	17·7	82·0
	Girls			
	N 157		N 81	
Upper Class	90·0	10·0	72·7	27·3
Lower Class	86·9	13·1	54·3	45·7

At least for children who enter English grammar schools and remain until the fifth or sixth forms, the influence of social origin appears to be eliminated in shaping occupational and social aspirations. The school is the decisive frame of reference rather

[1] Boys with fathers in occupations within the Registrar-General's classes I, II and IIIa (routine non-manual).
[2] Compiled from Tables III and IV, W. Liversidge, loc. cit.

than the family or peer group. In this sense at least the English grammar school can claim to be 'democratic'; the American high school, by contrast, fails to reduce the force of the social-class system in determining the life chances of the young.

Chapter Three

THE INVENTION OF THE ADOLESCENT

THE adolescent was invented at the same time as the steam-engine. The principal architect of the latter was Watt in 1765, of the former Rousseau in 1762. Having invented the adolescent, society has been faced with two major problems: how and where to accommodate him in the social structure, and how to make his behaviour accord with the specifications. For two centuries English society has been involved in the problem of defining and clarifying the concept of precocity.

Rousseau defined the adolescent, but he evaded the problem of his location in society by consigning him with his tutor to the wilderness. He belittled childhood as a phase of development: the first twelve years of life could be abandoned to 'negative education'. But puberty, he claimed, 'is the second birth I spoke of; then it is that man really enters upon life; henceforth no human passion is a stranger to him. Our efforts (in education) so far have been child's play, now they are of the greatest importance. The period when education is usually finished is just the time to begin . . .'[1]

The tailor, the publisher, the social reformer and the educator came to Rousseau's assistance: they began in the later eighteenth and early nineteenth centuries to cater for a specific age-group of 'young persons', neither children nor adults. Instead of wearing imitation-adult clothing, young people at the end of the eighteenth century had their distinctive uniform, including 'long trousers', which actually anticipated the grown-up fashions of the future.[2] School stories such as *Tom Brown* (1856) and *Eric, or Little by*

[1] *Emile*, Bk. IV.
[2] See J. Laver, *Children's Fashions of the Nineteenth Century* (1951).

Little (1858), *The Boys' Own Paper* (from 1879) and *Stalky and Co.* (1903) addressed themselves to, and helped to create, a specifically (middle-class) adolescent world.

Reforms of the penal system and of factory conditions also distinguished 'young persons' from children on the one hand and from adults on the other. Mary Carpenter argued strenuously that young persons should be distinguished from adults by the law courts, should suffer penalties appropriate to their years, and receive corrective treatment in special, juvenile reformatories.[1] The Youthful Offenders Act of 1854 enabled magistrates to treat young offenders and adult criminals differently. The Factory Acts of 1833 and 1847 distinguished the age-group 13–18 as needing protection from the full rigours of the adult world and restricted their hours of labour.

Social legislation and changing social conventions *made* the adolescent. Areas of experience and knowledge were now designated 'adult', from which the less-than-adult must be shielded. The early acquaintance with birth and especially with death were no longer considered essential to a child's education:[2] these were adult matters from which the young should be carefully excluded. The young were now kept from the room in which confinement or death occurred:[3] more spacious and elaborate architecture made it possible to segregate the young from such adult concerns.

And yet before his redefinition in the nineteenth century the adolescent had not necessarily been wholly integrated into the life of the adult world—or at least, in the case of upper-class children, into the world of adults who were their social equals. Indeed, it was the great achievement of the eighteenth century to rescue middle- and upper-class youth from the world of their social inferiors. For a time, at the end of the century, there was a powerful middle- and upper-class movement to save them from

[1] See Mary Carpenter, 'On the Non-Imprisonment of Children', *Transactions of the National Association for the Promotion of Social Science* (1864) and *Reformatory Schools for the Children of the Perishing and Dangerous Classes* (1851).

[2] For examples of parents deliberately confronting their children with death see *The Memoirs of Thomas Holcroft* (1816) and Mrs Sherwood, *The Fairchild Family* (1818). In both fathers took children on an educational visit to the gibbet.

[3] Working-class housing conditions in the eighteenth and early nineteenth centuries made early acquaintance with birth and with death extremely likely, indeed, inevitable. See *Report on the Employment of Women and Children in Agriculture* (1843), p. 21 and J. Hole, *The Homes of the Working Classes* (1866), pp. 12–13.

relegation to the marginal world of menials and domestic servants and to bring them more intimately into the lives of their own families. This experiment was incongruous with the needs of a rapidly changing social order; and in the nineteenth century upper-class youths were again ejected from their families—but now into the protected world of the public school.

In the later eighteenth century adolescence was not only redefined, as a distinct phase of the life cycle, but socially re-classified. Little distinction had been made hitherto between older children and adolescents: they sat together in the schools and were subject to similar discipline. They were not distinguished in dress, in the games they played, in the books they read. Formerly the upper-class young had been classed with servants and apprentices—often, indeed, they *were* apprentices, if they were younger sons. They were socially and often geographically remote from their elders; the elaboration of domestic architecture had made it possible to seclude them from the orbit of adult affairs, in the children's parlour or the 'Red Room'; although, as they advanced in years, they were more often to be found at the stable door. The tutor or governess who might supervise their lives was a menial, treated as such, a member of the servants' hall, as many have bitterly testified in their memoirs.[1]

The infants of upper- and middle-class families were suckled by the wives of peasants and labourers. Powerful voices testified to, and attacked, this practice: Defoe criticized the upper-class mother on this score, as did Priestley,[2] Whitchurch[3] and Rousseau. David Williams described her as 'the most unnatural brute in creation'.[4]

But older children were also permitted an easy relationship and familiarity with servants. Locke was issuing a warning against a widespread situation when he advised the parent to keep his child free 'from the taint of servants'. 'And there is another great inconvenience, which children receive from the ill examples which they meet with, among the meaner servants. They are wholly, if possible, to be kept from such conversation: for the contagion of these ill precedents, both in civility and

[1] See Joseph Priestley, *Observations on Education* (1788), p. 53, George Chapman, *Treatise on Education* (1790), p. 35, Anne Bronte, *Agnes Grey* (1847).
[2] J. Priestley, op. cit., p. 91.
[3] J. W. Whitchurch, *Essay upon Education* (1772), p. 32.
[4] David Williams, *Lectures on Education* (1789), vol. I, p. 16.

virtue horribly infects children, as often as they come within reach of it. They frequently learn from unbred and debauched servants such language, untowardly tricks and vices, as otherwise they would possibly be ignorant of all their lives.'[1] Defoe similarly complained of the country squire who 'educates his sons at the stable door, instead of the grammar school, and his huntsman is Head Tutor'.[2] But even when he educated them at the grammar or public school he was unperturbed by the social mixture they would encounter. It was not until the middle of the nineteenth century that the 'social difficulty' which the Taunton Commission described caused the decay of grammar schools as the middle classes withdrew their sons from inferior social contacts.[3]

The young were consigned to the company of servants because they were socially classified with servants. This was not a situation peculiar to England. Ariès has pointed to the similarity of conditions in France and England: 'Le *Book of Common Prayer* de 1549 fait une obligation aux chefs de famille de veiller à l'instruction religieuse de tous les enfants de la maison, c'est-à-dire aux *children, servants and prentices*. Les serviteurs et apprentis sont assimilés aux enfants de la famille. Ils s'amusaient entre eux à des jeux de gamins.'[4]

The relegation of the young to the world of their social inferiors (and often to inferior living quarters and even an inferior diet) was commented on adversely by some seventeenth- and eighteenth-century writers. Locke reproved parents for their aloofness towards their children, for a 'constant stiffness, and a mien of authority to them all their lives.'[5] He complained: 'And why those, who live in the country, should not take them (their children) with them, when they make visits of civility to their neighbours, I do not know'.[6] Locke's recommendations were clearly of a revolutionary nature.

[1] John Locke, *Thoughts concerning Education*, sec. 68.
[2] D. Defoe, *The Compleat English Gentleman* (1890 ed.), pp. 238–9. See also R. L. Edgeworth, *Practical Education* (1789), vol. I, ch. 4 and J. Priestley, op. cit., p. 91.
[3] See *Report of the Schools Inquiry Commission* (1868), vol. 9, pp. 497–8.
[4] Philippe Ariès, *L'Enfant et La Vie Familiale* (1960), pp. 447–8. Ariès constantly reverts to this theme, to 'une ambiguité entre le valet subalterne et le collaborateur plus relevé . . . Une pareille ambiguité existait entre l'enfant—ou le très jeune homme—et le serviteur' (p. 411).
[5] John Locke, op. cit., sec. 96.
[6] Ibid., sec. 70.

A century later the same complaints were still being made. David Williams asserted that in the homes of the gentry 'The father's attention is divided by the mercenary politics of parties, and the qualities of brutes: mothers are occupied by frivolous plans of fatiguing dissipation; by anxiety to give point or wit to cards, for insipid, importunate visitors, or messages for the health of dogs. But of their children they know only their persons, and reputation in the house.'[1] Williams complained of fathers who knew their dogs better than their children; he commented acidly on the formalized, ritualistic separation of child and adult worlds. 'In almost all the families I know'—and as a private tutor his acquaintance was extensive—'children are ushered to their parents at appointed hours and with certain ceremonies.' The contact was not only formal but of exceedingly brief duration.

Susan Sibbald, the fifth daughter of Dr Thomas Mein, R.N., described such ceremonies as practised at her home in Fowey in the 1790s. The apartments and routine of the children were quite separate from those of the adults of the household. The 'children's parlour' and the schoolroom were in a remote, upper part of the house.

Child and adult worlds briefly converged and made nominal contact each day by special arrangement. The children were attired for a ceremonial appearance each evening in the drawing-room. 'We had to be dressed out for the occasion, in coloured silk slips, and muslin frocks, which were very suitable, as the moment we entered the drawing-room, after our formal curtsies, we had to sit up all in a row, and we were constantly told, "be silent, and look pretty, as children should be seen and not heard".'[2] The children were not long detained in this alien sphere. 'After a while, at a bow to the governess from my mother, we again made our curtsies at the door, and were marched off to our part of the house, to our great delight.'

'Integration': An Interlude

In the later eighteenth century there occurred a vigorous, widespread and self-conscious movement to enfold the children

[1] D. Williams, *Lectures on Education* (1789), vol. 2, p. 291.
[2] F. P. Hett (ed.), *Memoirs of Susan Sibbald 1738–1812* (1926), p. 6.

of the gentry and the professional middle classes within their own families. They were sent less often to other people's families—as apprentices or as boarders while they attended a public school.[1] There was a revival of domestic education, but domestic education with a difference, in which parents played the role of tutor.

Hired tutors might also be employed as auxiliaries, but the main burden of teaching the younger children was urged upon the mother, and of the older children and adolescents, particularly the boys, upon the father. 'Teaching' was to be interpreted widely: the education of the young should be accomplished by associating them with the central concerns and business of the household. This movement occurred broadly between the 1760s and the 1830s. The refashioned public school of Arnold's day finally took over the burden with which many families had struggled. Both the late-eighteenth-century solution of integration, and the mid-nineteenth-century solution of segregation in the reformed (and socially exclusive) public schools, gave to the middle- and upper-class young an importance and status which they had not hitherto enjoyed. It is true that domestic education brought the young more immediately under parental authority, but they were no longer relegated, with but little concern, to the world of menials. They were now at the centre of the household, often involved in its most important affairs.

Domestic education, conducted by parents, was urged in order to rescue the young from contaminating contacts with servants, tutors and coevals. These considerations were supported by the psychological theories prevailing in the eighteenth century regarding innate individual differences: only parents could be aware of the special, inborn characteristics of their children and cater especially for them.

Locke had described the ideal private tutor but was conscious of his rarity. He would be a cultivated gentleman with wide experience of men and affairs, able 'to fashion the carriage, and

---

[1] Sending the well-born to *other people's* families for their education had a long tradition extending back to the medieval world. Chivalric education had been given in baronial households: 'The pupils in the first instance were wards of the head of the house, but their number was increased by the sons and daughters of his great vassals and others of similar rank.' See J. W. Adamson, 'Education' in F. J. C. Hearnshaw (ed.), *Medieval Contributions to Modern Civilization* (1922), p. 209.

form the mind; to settle in his pupil good habits, and the principles of virtue and wisdom'. Scholarship and learning were less important than knowledge of the world and polite society.

Locke was aware that few tutors measured up to his ideal; and widespread dissatisfaction with the personal qualities of private tutors encouraged the advocacy of fathers as tutors. Defoe regarded tutors as 'murtherers of a child's moralls'[1] and the complaint of the servility of tutors was widespread in the eighteenth century. Their equivocal role within the family made it difficult for them to be otherwise;[2] they were, said David Williams, 'the most servile and accommodating order in the community'.[3] Priestley dwelt on the harmful effects on the pupil of seeing a man of liberal education 'treated on the footing of a servant or a chaplain';[4] George Chapman deplored the undue dependence of tutors on the parents of their pupils, on whom they relied not only for their present subsistence, but for their future establishment, since their posts were necessarily temporary.[5]

Edward Hyde, the first earl of Clarendon, stated his opinion in the late-seventeenth century that education at school would solve the problem of contamination by social inferiors at home: 'I must rather recommend the education in public schools and communities,' he wrote in his *Two Dialogues on Education*, 'than under governors and preceptors in the private families of their parents, where are only one or two more of the children of that family; and where the vices of all the servants are every day exposed to them, with too much of their company, which no care in those places can prevent'. But many voices, including Locke's, protested that the young were as likely to be contaminated by their peers as by their tutors, that they had nothing to learn from their coevals but vice, 'malapertness, tricking and violence'. The most acceptable solution seemed to be the assumption of the role of tutor by the father—a proposal not altogether unrealistic

---

[1] See *The Compleat English Gentleman*.
[2] See Pillans, 'On Domestic Education', *Transactions* N.A.P.S.Sc. (1859). The tutor occupied 'a sort of debateable ground, an isthmus that connects the higher and lower parts of the (domestic) establishment'.
[3] *Lectures on Education* (1789), vol. I, p. 58.
[4] *Observations on Education* (1788), p. 53.
[5] See George Chapman, *Treatise on Education* (1790), p. 35.

in an age when wealth and high social status still generally implied leisure.[1]

Those educationists who stressed inborn differences of temperament and talent tended to support the idea of domestic education conducted by parents as the form most likely to take them fully into account. The controversy regarding the significance for child development of the environment on the one hand, or of innate disposition on the other, was one of the major preoccupations of eighteenth-century philosophers and educationists. By the end of the century the environmentalist viewpoint of Hartley and Helvetius generally prevailed, finding one of its most extreme and uncompromising expressions in Godwin's *Political Justice*. But hitherto, deeply ingrained or innate differences of personality and ability had been generally stressed.

Even Locke, although he rejected innate ideas, recognized deep-seated differences in attitude, temper and disposition; and it was this aspects of his thought which was often seized upon by writers in the early and mid-eighteenth century. (It was not until Locke's sensationalist philosophy was represented by Helvetius in his *Treatise on Man* (1772) as applicable to temperament as well as ideas, that Locke was seen by English educationists as the champion of environment against innate endowment.)

It is true that Locke had written that children were 'as white paper, or wax, to be moulded and fashioned as one pleases'; but he had also maintained that 'We must not hope to change original tempers, nor make the gay pensive and grave; nor the melancholy sportive, without spoiling them. God has stamped certain characters on men's minds, which, like their shapes, may perhaps be a little mended, but can hardly be transformed into the contrary.'[2] Many minor theorists of the eighteenth century

---

[1] Clearly, however, it could not be a universal remedy. R. L. Edgeworth was one of its major advocates, but asked: 'How are the vast numbers who are themselves occupied in public and professional pursuits . . . to educate their families when they have not time to attend them? . . . if in such situations parents were to attempt to educate their children at home, they would harass themselves, and probably spoil their children irrecoverably' (*Practical Education*, vol. 2, pp. 147–8). Cf. David Williams *Lectures on Education*, vol. I: 'Such a revolution in manners as would leave parents at leisure to educate their children is hardly to be attempted' (p. 154).

[2] See *Thoughts concerning Education*, sec. 66. Cf. *Of the Conduct of Human Understanding*, sec. 2. 'Among men of equal education there is great inequality of parts. And the woods of America, as well as the schools of Athens, produce men of several abilities in the same kind.'

echoed these views. 'Children differ from each other, no less in the singularities of genius, than in the features of the face,' wrote James Whitchurch in the 1770s.[1] Such views led to the advocacy of highly individual tuition. 'Scarcely two children,' said Locke, 'can be instructed by the same method.'

Helvetius and his disciples, who recognized no natural differences in children, could with easy minds relegate the young to the schools, in which mass methods of instruction prevailed. As David Williams observed: 'On Helvetius's principle there would be no blockhead but from the negligence of the instructor.' As an experienced teacher he was familiar with the recalcitrance of human nature as well as its plasticity; he was not convinced that all had the same inborn capacity. 'I apprehend the doctrine of innate ideas to be nonsense, and that all ideas are derived from education. I think, however, that nature has not given all men the same capacity of intellectual and moral improvement.'[2] On such grounds he opposed the 'mechanic order' of the schools and advocated domestic tuition.

Whitchurch took up a similar position: 'The modes of domestic education admit of infinite variations, and may be expressly adapted to each peculiarity of genius that is discernible in a young person.'[3] Barclay argued likewise: 'As every tree must be planted in a soil proper to its kind, and requires particular culture, so our various tempers and dispositions demand each a different manner of instruction and improvement.' He had no confidence that the schools of the day could provide teaching appropriate to individual needs, and saw the only hope in more extensive domestic education. 'We can no more be all equally wise, than equally rich or fair . . . What can be more ridiculous, than the general way of recommending the same task, and expecting the same application and progress from the several children that meet together in a grammar-school? as if all were precisely the same in genius, and had equally a turn for Latin and Greek.' It was useless to blame schoolmasters 'for what is not in the power of any but nature to correct'.[4]

There were critics of domestic education, of plans to

---

[1] James Whitchurch, *Essay upon Education* (1772), p. 119.
[2] D. Williams, *Treatise on Education* (1774), p. 64.
[3] J. Whitchurch, op. cit., p. 119.
[4] James Barclay, *Treatise on Education* (1743), p. 39.

incorporate the child in the closed world of the family. Robert Southey[1] and Mary Wollstonecraft,[2] like Helvetius, urged the value of finding one's own level among one's contemporaries. In order to achieve the maximum effect of education by and with coevals, Helvetius would have severely limited contacts with adults: teachers would be remote supervisors, parents would be totally banished: 'It is necessary that he (the pupil) be almost always absent from the paternal dwelling; and that he does not return in the vacations and holidays, to catch again, from conversation with people of the world, the vices his fellow-pupils had effaced.'[3]

But in 1762, in his *Emile*, Rousseau put the weight of his authority not only behind domestic education, but behind domestic education conducted by the father. Although he deprived Emile of his parents, he was of opinion that ideally the father should be the tutor. (This was one way in which a man might extend his 'freedom', by making himself independent of hired assistants or substitutes.[4]) 'Poverty, pressure of business, mistaken social prejudices, none of these can excuse a man from his duty, which is to support and educate his own children.' 'What does this rich man do, this father of a family, compelled, so he says, to neglect his children? He pays another man to perform the duties which are his alone. Mercenary man! Do you expect to purchase a second father for your child? Do not deceive yourself; it is not even a master you have hired for him, it is a flunkey, who will soon train such another as himself.'[5]

These views found widespread support in England. 'No man,' echoed David Williams, 'is in all respects capable of educating a child, but the father of it; and hardly any consideration should ever take children out of my hands.' Williams, at least in his earlier writings in the 1770s, even went so far as to assert that there was no way of 'saving the nation, but by advising every man to recur to his natural duties and take care of his children.'

[1] See C. C. Southey (ed.), *Life and Correspondence of Robert Southey* (1849), vol. I, p. 79.
[2] See *Vindications of the Rights of Women* (1796), ch. 12.
[3] *A Treatise on Man*, Vol. 2, translated by W. Hooper (1777), p. 400.
[4] See *Emile*, Bk. 2. 'There is only one man who gets his own way—he who gets it single-handed.' Cf. *The Social Contract*, ch. 15: the free man would do his own governing: he would not have deputies to do it for him.
[5] *Emile*, Bk. 1.

He was aware that these sentiments might 'be considered visionary and impracticable, because parents in general are unfit for the undertaking'; but he was optimistic as he looked to the future. While schools ('as much like well-regulated families . . . as it is possible to make them') might be necessary for the time being, a generation of parents who had been more wisely educated in their youth might revert to the obvious and natural duties of parenthood. He looked forward to the time when schools would wither away: men would be 'capable of presiding in their families and educating their children; and render schools themselves unnecessary'.[1]

This late-eighteenth-century revival of domestic education must be seen as one manifestation of the greater concern for the young which marked the age, a new willingness to recognize and consider their unique personal needs. It is difficult to estimate the actual extent to which the young of middle- and upper-class English society were thus incorporated within their families in the later eighteenth and early nineteenth centuries. A high proportion of the eminent men of the eighteenth century, whose histories have been recorded in the *Dictionary of National Biography*, were educated at home. A quarter of those who were the sons of peers, and a third of those who were the sons of gentry, were educated domestically.[2] Contemporaries who urged even more domestic education pointed to the distinction of many of its products. (M. D. Hill attacked this method of evaluating domestic education on the grounds that genius would emerge regardless of the particular form of education employed.[3])

When Vicesimus Knox, headmaster of Tonbridge School, brought out a new edition of his book, *Liberal Education*, in 1795,[4] he conceded that 'perhaps in former editions I have expressed myself rather too strongly in preferring public to private education'. 'I have observed,' he wrote, 'that private tuition seems lately to have prevailed in this country more than ever'.[5] Charlotte Mason, looking back, in the later nineteenth

[1] *Treatise on Education* (1774), p. 27.
[2] See N. Hans, *New Trends in Eighteenth Century Education* (1951).
[3] See M. D. Hill, *Plans for the Government and Liberal Education of Boys, in Large Numbers* (1822), pp. 191–2.
[4] First published 1781.
[5] *Liberal Education* (1795 ed.), p. 263.

century, to the revival of domestic education in its new form, with father and mother as joint tutors, saw Rousseau as the principal inspiration of the movement: 'Under the spell of his teaching, people in the fashionable world, like that Russian Princess Galitzin, forsook society, and went off with their children to some quiet corner where they could devote every hour of the day, and every power they had, to the fulfilment of the duties which devolve upon parents. Courtly mothers retired from the world, sometimes left their husbands . . . that they might with their own lips instruct their children.'[1]

Richard Lovell Edgeworth, William Cobbett and James Mill are only three of the better known examples of the father-tutor of the period: their endeavours have been well documented by themselves or by their children. Their aim was not simply the formal instruction of their children, but their involvement in the total life of the household, their association with its adult concerns. This was an experiment in integration and incorporation of the young.

Maria Edgeworth has described how this social experiment worked under her father. His multifarious activities were no hindrance to his educational projects, for the very variety of his occupations 'assisted in affording him daily and hourly opportunities for giving instruction after his manner, without formal lectures or lessons. For instance, at the time when he was building or carrying on experiments or work of any sort, he constantly explained to his children whatever was doing or to be done . . .' This easy, informal association of the children with the concerns of the household caused 'animation (to) spread through the house by connecting children with all that was going on, and allowing them to join in thought or conversation with the grown-up people of the family . . . Both sympathy and emulation excited mental exertion in the most agreeable manner.'[2]

A spate of books offered a blue-print for the new-model integrated household.[3] Many of the fathers who were inspired to try the experiment doubtless did so perfunctorily after their

---

[1] Charlotte Mason, *Parents and Children* (1907 ed.), p. 2. Cf. Edmund Gosse, *Father and Son* (1907). Gosse's grandfather was inspired by Rousseau to educate his children in Snowdonia.

[2] *Memoirs of R. L. Edgeworth* (1821), ch. 8.

[3] E.g. Thomas Day, *Sandford and Merton* (1783), Mrs Sherwood, *The Fairchild Family* (1818), E. W. Benson, *Education at Home* (1824).

first bout of enthusiasm;[1] but others proved to be efficient teachers. John Keble and his brother were both educated by their father until they obtained Oxford scholarships at an early age; Edward Copleston, Provost of Oriel and later Bishop of Llandaff, was educated by his father until he obtained a scholarship at Corpus at the age of 15. Best known, of course, is the case of John Stuart Mill who was closely associated on terms of equality with his father's most eminent friends. James Mill made no attempt to exclude his son from his business interests and intellectual concerns; the boy conversed with Hume and Bentham; and when he became interested in political economy, Ricardo invited him to his house 'to walk with him in order to converse on the subject'.

On Cobbett's farm, taken deliberately to promote an experimental all-age socio-educational unit, the instinctive endowment and executive capacity of children and adults were directed towards the same reality. The children were not encouraged to have their own separate interests and pursuits, and their learning was not an unreal abstraction from real-life situations.

Cobbett has told how literacy developed as the handmaid of severely practical, adult considerations: 'The paying of the workpeople, the keeping of accounts, the referring to books, the writing and reading of letters; the everlasting mixture of amusement with book-learning, made me, almost to my own surprise, find, at the end of two years . . . that I had a parcel of scholars growing up about me . . . The calculations about the farming affairs forced arithmetic upon us: the use, the necessity of the thing, led to the study. By-and-by, we had to look into the laws, to know what to do about the highways, about the game, about the poor, and all rural and parochial affairs.'[2]

The integration of the middle-and upper-class household, the incorporation of the young into the world of their parents as a deliberate educational device, was an interlude in English social life extending over five or six decades. It is true that between 1864 and 1894 the proportion of Oxford and Cambridge undergraduates who came not from schools but from domestic education remained constant, at the not inconsiderable figure of

---

[1] See for example George Crabbe's conduct of his children's education: *Life of George Crabbe* (1834) by his son.
[2] William Cobbett, *Advice to Young Men* (1926 ed.), pp. 288-9.

12 per cent.[1] Nevertheless, as a large-scale movement, domestic education appears to have declined steeply in the 1830s: the reformed public schools took over.[2]

When Hill was writing in 1822 the movement seemed as vigorous as ever; only radically reformed schools, of the kind Hill was pioneering at Hazelwood, seemed likely to undermine it. But when Isaac Taylor wrote to champion the cause of domestic education in 1838, he realized that public education had finally triumphed. He did not seek to reverse this trend; only to plead that some boys needed individual attention and consideration which no school could give, and these 'should come under that very different and more intimate process of culture of which the home must be the scene'.[3]

The Changing Role of the Upper Class School

Both the new-type domestic education of the later eighteenth century and the new-type public school which superseded it in the nineteenth, gave to the young a status and importance which they had not hitherto enjoyed. In households like Cobbett's, James Mill's and Edgeworth's, the young had the satisfaction of intimate contact with and contributing to the important concerns of their seniors. In the remodelled public schools after the 1830s the young lived in a world more thoroughly interpenetrated by adults than had been the case in the virtually self-regulating schoolboy societies which had prevailed hitherto.

Before the 1830s the school had diminished the young; it stood for their relegation to an inferior position on the periphery of society. Often it was looked on as a last and desperate resort for hard cases, or as the only hope for younger sons. Attendance even at the major schools did not automatically confer high

---

[1] See *Report of the Schools Inquiry Commission* (1868), vol. I, appendix 7, for the position at the earlier date. Out of returns made by 2,403 undergraduates, 278 were found to have been educated domestically. For 30 years later see *Report of the Royal Commission on Secondary Education* (1895), vol. 8, pp. 426–7. Out of 5,662 undergraduates, 646 had been educated at home.

[2] See also the author's articles 'Decline of the Educative Family', *Universities Quarterly* (1960), 14, and 'Middle-Class Families and Schools 1780–1880', *Sociological Review* (1959), 7.

[3] Isaac Taylor, *Home Education* (1838), pp. 19–20. For a full discussion of the issues presented above, see the author's 'Two Educational Controversies in Eighteenth-Century England', *Paedagogica Historica* (1962), 2.

social status, as it has for the past hundred years. As an age-grade organization the eighteenth-century public school can be seen largely as the product of frustrations and blockages within the kinship system: while the Tony Lumpkins, who had estates to inherit, had no need of school education,[1] their younger brothers had.

Eisenstadt has argued that one category of age-grade institution is that which arises when 'the "inferior" members of the family unit tend to over-emphasize their mutual solidarity *vis-à-vis* the older generations, instead of almost totally subordinating it to the overall solidarity of the total family unit.'[2] Roughly, the boys' public school before the 1830s (and the girls' after the 1860s) accord with this analysis. It was the repository for an outsider group, potentially deviant and revolutionary. Since the 1830s it has had a contrary role: a repository for 'insiders', presided over by masters who are the social equals or inferiors, seldom or never the social superiors of their pupils, it has automatically conferred, or held the promise of, high status; instead of constituting a potentially revolutionary social force, it has become the bulwark of social stability and continuity.

While, as Vicesimus Knox complained, there were parents who sent their boys to a public school principally to make influential contacts which would help them in later life,[3] the sons of the gentry and well-to-do professional men gained a more dubious advantage from a public school education. In 1736 Robert Ainsworth rebuked 'persons of good estate who . . . run so great a hazard to have the beautiful image (of their children) spoiled, and the whole work effaced . . . Here children of good and bad education (upbringing), and good and bad tempers, being huddled promiscuously together, it may be rather feared the bad may infect the good, than hoped the good may reform the bad.'[4] Only when the family was itself inadequate, or the young man wholly intractable, should the risk of a public school education

[1] See *She Stoops to Conquer* (1773), Act 1, Sc. i. Mrs Hardcastle: 'My son is not to live by his learning. I don't think a boy needs much learning to inherit fifteen hundred a year.'

[2] S. N. Eisenstadt, *From Generation to Generation* (1956), p. 53.

[3] V. Knox, *Liberal Education* (1795), vol. 2, p. 30: 'a son, in such cases, has usually been instructed at home, to pay a servile deference to those of his school-fellows who are likely to be distinguished by future rank or fortune.' Cf. Maria Edgeworth, *Patronage* (1813).

[4] See R. Ainsworth, *The Most Natural and Easy Way of Instruction* (1736).

be incurred; as Edgeworth advised: 'to a public school, as to a general infirmary for mental disease, all desperate subjects are sent, as a last resource.'[1]

It was the younger sons of men of property, who had no access to superior statuses through the kinship system, who needed a public, as opposed to a private, education. They were to be found as apprentices, public-school boys, and undergraduates. Swift, in his *Essay on Education*, lamented the failure of eldest sons to seek an education in the schools and universities; Defoe similarly regretted the situation and attempted to fill in the statistical details: 'Of thirty thousand families of noblemen and gentlemen of estate which may be reckoned up in this kingdom, I venture to say there is not two hundred of their eldest sons at a time to be found in both our universities. At the same time you will find ten times that number of their younger sons.'[2]

Apprentices, public-school boys and undergraduates were a marginal race, their status at the best ambiguous. They were a byword for turbulence. A public education was seen by many in the eighteenth century as a threat to tradition and established order: Defoe knew the argument of the Tory squire that a public education unsettled young men and unfitted them for the duties of estate management; Whitchurch advised against a public education on similar grounds.[3]

Public-school boys had a reputation for restlessness, insubordination and even violent rebellion no less than apprentices. (Inadequate supervision is not a complete explanation; apprentices were commonly over-supervised.) Winchester, Rugby and Eton were the scene of repeated and ugly disturbances in the late-eighteenth and early-nineteenth centuries, which were settled only by the intervention of the army. In 1768 a revolt at Eton was led by the praeposters, in 1783 a revolt against the headmaster resulted in considerable damage to property. In 1818 disturbances at Winchester were dealt with by the army. By the second quarter of the nineteenth century, as the public schools changed not only their character and internal organization, but their social function, the revolts died out: the last revolt at Eton

[1] M. and R. L. Edgeworth, *Practical Education* (1789), vol. 2, p. 150.
[2] D. Defoe, *The Compleat English Gentleman*.
[3] J. W. Whitchurch, *An Essay upon Education* (1772), p. 103.

occurred in 1832; the last of the revolts by public-school boys was at Marlborough College in 1851.[1] The eighteenth-century public school was a hostile, outsider age-grade organization, 'An enormous society of boys between the ages of 8 and 18 governed by an unwritten code of its own making, an almost free republic of 100, 200, or 500 members . . .'[2]

After the 1830s, when Arnold and other reforming head-masters changed the nature of the English public schools, boys were not abandoned to their own devices; they associated to a greater extent with their schoolmasters, the house system was modelled on family life. (Boarders were not generally incorporated into Harrow School until 1820–50; many had previously lived in the town, beyond the headmaster's authority.[3]) But of greater significance was the fact that attendance at a public school no longer implied inferior status (as a younger son or a 'hard case'); as the public schools set out deliberately to achieve social exclusiveness, often quite contrary to their founders' intentions, they came automatically to confer high status on their inmates. The son of the self-made industrialist was, indeed, guaranteed a higher social status than his father.

The exclusion of social inferiors was the great achievement of public-school headmasters of the mid-nineteenth century. Vaughan at Harrow, Kennedy at Shrewsbury, and Arnold at Rugby, set out quite systematically to exclude local boys, generally of inferior social rank, from their schools. Their strategems and legal battles met with great success. Ancient endowed grammar schools which failed to achieve such exclusive-ness—Batley, Keighley, Kingsbridge, Bideford and Crewkerne, for example—sank to the level of elementary schools;[4] Aldenham, Highgate and Sherborne were reported by the Taunton Com-mission to be prospering because they could offer well-to-do parents the assurance of elevating social contacts for their sons. The new proprietary schools like Clifton and Bath Proprietary College applied a rigorous test of gentility to all applicants for admission. Men who had themselves been educated at local and socially mixed grammar schools earlier in the century, were

[1] For a summary of these incidents and a general discussion of their sociological significance, see Philippe Ariès, op. cit., p. 356.
[2] E. Halévy, *England in 1815* (London 1949), pp. 535–6.
[3] See E. D. Laborde, *Harrow School* (1948), pp. 174–5.
[4] See *Report of the Schools Inquiry Commission* (1868), vol. 9, p. 151.

seeking more exclusive establishments for their sons by the eighteen-fifties.

Upper-class schools for girls experienced a contrary change of function between the late-eighteenth and the late-nineteenth centuries. At the former date they gave enhanced status to the daughters of well-to-do farmers who aspired to the society of the gentry; at the latter they functioned to a great extent as a repository for superfluous daughters who could ever less find acceptable accommodation within the kinship system. Educated women of the later eighteenth century—with the notable exception of Mary Wollstonecraft, who was sternly disapproved of by the other blue-stockings of the day—were remarkable for their conservatism and even reactionary social views. Mary Delany, Elizabeth Carter, Elizabeth Montagu, Hester Lynch Thrale, Fanny Burney—none throughout her remarkably long life sought to upset the traditional balance of society. Hester Chapone,[1] ('the bluest of the Blues') and Hannah More[2] breathed no hint of criticism of the established social order in their published works. A century later upper- and middle-class women used their education for deviant social purposes: their schools were an expression of their social difficulties, not of their social ascendance.

The late-eighteenth century private schools for girls stood for the enhancement of status; the middle-class girls' schools a century later were symptoms of status frustration: they were the background to a militant feminist movement culminating in the Suffragettes. Upper-class girls of the eighteenth century were, in the main, educated within the family; but when the family was itself seeking to change its social status, the teaching of appropriate behaviour was beyond its scope. The multiplication of polite seminaries for the daughters of aspiring farmers, enriched by the agrarian revolution and the French wars, was adversely commented upon by contemporary writers.[3] While their superior education might unfit them for their duties in the farm kitchen, it would prepare them to appear to advantage in county circles. If they failed to marry, the extended kinship system could still

[1] See *Strictures on the Modern System of Female Education.*
[2] See *Letters to a New Married Lady* and *Letters on the Improvement of the Mind.*
[3] See Clara Reeve, *Plans of Education* (1792), T. Day, *Sandford and Merton*, vol. 3, pp. 300–3. Also Ivy Pinchbeck, *Women Workers in the Industrial Revolution* (1930), p. 38.

usually give them work and significance as companions and governesses in the households of their sisters, brothers and aunts.

The mid-Victorian upper-class family was less able and willing to shoulder the burden of superfluous spinsters; there was little paid professional employment for them to undertake. They 'came out' and were married off by seniority. Jane Austen made the younger Bennet sisters in *Pride and Prejudice* rebel against this custom; Charlotte Bronte in *Shirley* described the competition for husbands and the consequent frustrations in mid-century middle-class families: 'They scheme, they plot, they dress to ensnare husbands . . . Fathers . . . order them to stay at home. What do they expect them to do at home?' Increasingly they found their way into schools, and even the universities.[1] With education they could force the social and political changes which would provide them with the roles, status and significance which were denied them.

The Concept of Precocity

The definition of the adolescent implied a theory of the rate of progress towards maturity. This rate was to be retarded (or allowed to find its hypothetically 'natural' level) in order to insert between childhood and adulthood a discrete and distinctive phase of human growth and development. 'En ce début du XIX*e* siècle,' observes Ariès, 'on se méfie de la precocité.'[2]

Locke had advised the instructor of youth: 'The sooner you treat him as a man, the sooner he will be one.' This was the obvious goal of education in his day, the earliest possible achievement of adult attitudes and behaviour; the only quarrel concerned the method of achieving it. (Locke saw domestic education as the most powerful instrument for his purpose; the earl of Clarendon saw the school—but the intention was the same: 'There is so much benefit arising from the mutual conversation of many children together . . . that we seldom see a boy continue long of childish understanding in those companies.'[3])

[1] Miss Buss became headmistress of the North London Collegiate School in 1850, Miss Beale the first principal of the Ladies' College, Cheltenham, in 1858. The G.P.D.S.C. was founded in 1872. Emily Davies moved her college from Hitchin to Girton in 1873.

[2] Philippe Ariès, op. cit., p. 253.

[3] See *Dialogues on Education*.

In accordance with his sensationalist philosophy, whereby knowledge and understanding were seen to grow and expand from experience and sense impressions, Locke advocated for the pupil a rich and various social life. The boy should be introduced early to polite society, for thereby 'you will insensibly raise his mind above the usual amusements of youth'. This philosophy, and the practical advice which derived from it, had a large and influential following in the eighteenth century. Isaac Watts asked whether we did not 'attain a variety of sensible and intellectual ideas by the sensations of outward objects,'[1] and, like Locke, proceeded to commend in education the fullest possible social life for the young pupil. 'Where time and fortune allow it,' he argued, 'young people should be led into company at proper seasons, should be carried abroad to see the fields, and the woods, and the rivers, the buildings, towns and cities distant from their own dwelling; they should be entertained with the sight of strange birds, beasts, fishes, insects, vegetables, and productions both of nature and art of every kind.' He warmly approved the practice of mothers who, 'when there was company in the parlour . . . brought her son among them . . . Thus, by enjoying the advantages of society above the level of his own age and understanding, he was always aspiring to imitation.' Other educationists argued likewise: 'If ever you wish to see your children possessed of manly virtues,' wrote Whitchurch, 'and become useful members of society, teach them to act like men while they are still children.'

It was one of the paradoxes of Rousseau that he recommended the postponement of maturity[2] by the means least calculated to achieve it. It is true that the domestic education he recommended was far from the sociable variety proposed by Locke and his followers; but even those who, like Edgeworth, responded most ardently to his educational theories, were seldom prepared to accept his profound misanthropy and isolate the adolescent from all human society. In the event, they lacked the courage of Rousseau's convictions. The adolescent, having been invented,

[1] See *Improvement of the Mind* (1741–51) (1804 ed.), p. 23.
[2] 'Exercise his body, his limbs, his senses, his strength, but keep his mind idle as long as you can . . . leave childhood to ripen in your children. In a word, beware of giving anything they need today if it can be deferred without danger to tomorrow' (*Emile*).

was difficult to accommodate in the home: in constant interaction with his elders he refused to mark time. Domestic education
was a forcing house of early intellectual and social attainment;
it was not an appropriate instrument for prolonging and
elaborating adolescence as a distinct phase of development.

The very success of domestic education, particularly the kind
that Locke had urged, was undermining the new ideal of arrested
social growth. The exposure of boys of 14 and 15 to the
social world of adults, maintained Knox in the 1780s, produced
'multitudes of beardless boys assuming airs of manhood, and
practising many vices, to obtain the appellation of men.' This
was the outcome, he thought, of false educational doctrines
which had led (upper-class) parents to conclude that 'innocence,
modesty, submission to superiors . . . are signs of stupidity.'[1]
This is not a theme in the writing of educationists before this
time; in the last two decades of the eighteenth century it frequently recurs. 'We now endeavour,' lamented Priestley in 1788,
'to give children all the exterior polish they can receive, as soon
as possible; we bring them very early into mixed company, and
are proud of their bearing a part in conversation with grown
men and women.'[2] Priestley would have preferred their erstwhile
segregation in subordination, when they were seldom brought
into company, and so 'contracted a bashfulness which, by
disqualifying them from appearing to advantage in what is called
polite company, made them rather shun it.'

'Nature' was invoked as the measure of the proper rate of
progress towards social and intellectual maturity. Rousseau and
his followers saw the individual as a part of nature, evolving
according to its laws, rather than as a product of society. Botanical
analogies were widely employed: social and intellectual development were conceived as being of the same order as organic
growth. 'The minds of children,' asserted Louisa Hoare, 'as
their bodies, are not to be forced. We are to follow the leadings
of nature.' Parents were impatient and untrustworthy botanists,
anxious for earlier blooms than nature intended. 'Premature
acquirements, premature quickness of mind, premature feeling,
and even premature propriety of conduct, are not often the
evidence of real strength of character, and are rarely followed by

[1] V. Knox, op. cit., sec. 36, 'On Knowing the World at an Early Age'.
[2] *Observations on Education* (1788), p. 57.

corresponding fruits in future life.'[1] Parents were ignorant of what was natural and proper to each stage of children's growth, said M. D. Hill: 'Education rather resembles agriculture, and the tutor must take care that he does not fall into the error of plucking up the springs of knowledge which he has planted, in his anxiety to ascertain if they have taken root.'[2]

'Adult' social and intellectual skills were common in boys who enjoyed a domestic education of the reformed variety in the later eighteenth and in the nineteenth centuries. John Stuart Mill's 'precocity' is only one of the more outstanding and best documented examples. Bertrand Russell's upbringing in the home of his grandfather seems to have been as unsociable as Rousseau would have wished; but his intellectual development was such as Locke would have approved. 'I was a solitary, shy, priggish youth,' he recalls. 'I had no experience of the social pleasures of boyhood and did not miss them. But I liked mathematics, and mathematics was suspect because it had no ethical content.'[3]

Schoolmasters could be trusted more completely than parents to impede the progress of the young towards maturity. Sir Stephen King-Hall has illustrated the difference in his reminiscences of his Edwardian boyhood. His mother encouraged him to take part in the life and interests of adults: 'from an early age I was allowed to be present amongst the grown-ups and to take part in conversation. No book or newspaper I wanted to read was denied me . . . This was all very well in the family circle, but it was not a good preparation for life in a world where it was considered an offence to know better than your elders if you were a child.' His schoolmasters had a different scale by which they measured the evolution of the young: 'What they said—amongst other things—can be summed up in the one word "precocious". It was sometimes qualified. I was "very precocious", or "rather precocious", or "somewhat precocious", and once I was "unpleasantly precocious".'[4]

The adolescent was inappropriately located within the family: the characteristics which had been ascribed to him could more certainly be produced in the school. The nineteenth-century

[1] See Louisa Hoare, *Hints for the Improvement of Early Education* (1822 ed.).
[2] *Public Education* (1822), pp. 208–9.
[3] Bertrand Russell, *Portraits from Memory* (1956), p. 9.
[4] Stephen King-Hall, 'On Being Precocious', *The Listener* (2 August 1956), pp. 67–8.

public school redefined, and, indeed, re-made the adolescent. Children were excluded and placed in preparatory departments after the 1830s. Before this time public schools had contained boys of all ages from 8 to 19. Charles Lamb and Leigh Hunt entered Christ's Hospital at the age of 6; Lord Brougham and Walter Scott went to Edinburgh High School at the age of 7; Grote to Charterhouse at 10; both Palmerston and Gladstone went to Eton at the age of 11. Even the early 'preparatory' schools such as Cheam often prepared their pupils for the universities as well as the public schools. Windlesham House at Brighton, founded in 1837 by Lieutenant C. R. Malden, R.N., appears to have been the first purely preparatory school of the modern kind. The Grange School, Stevenage, was founded in the same year; Twyford and Temple Grove evolved slowly into preparatory schools. By the mid-century the public schools had become, in the main, the fortress of the adolescent proper.

And yet Arnold never came to terms with the new invention: he would not have the school prolong adolescence, but shorten it. He wished to reduce to the minimum the gap between childhood and manhood, for the gap was likely to be filled with grave moral dangers. He insisted that staff and pupils should live as nearly as possible as friends and equals; his sermons and addresses to the boys were in adult language. As he told the assembled school: 'The danger of the intermediate state between childhood and manhood is too often this, that whilst on the one point of teachableness, the change runs on too fast, on the other three, of wisdom, of unselfishness, and of thoughtfulness, it proceeds much too slowly . . . If the change from childhood to manhood can be hastened safely, it ought to be hastened; and it is a sin in everyone not to hasten it.'[1]

The new philosophy and objectives of the public school were more typically expressed by Warden Sewell of Radley College: 'How I dread mannikizing a boy. It is to me just as bad as opening an egg and finding an advanced chicken inside it . . . What say you to a baby with whiskers, or mustachios? No, keep boys boys—children children—young men young men. I remember Arthur Gordon repeating the story of one of the American ministers—a very sensible man. The thing which delighted him

---

[1] See J. J. Findlay, *Arnold of Rugby* (1925), p. 149 for a sermon preached by Arnold in August 1839.

and astonished him most in England was the boys. They had no boys in America. They are all premature men; they never pass through the intermediate stage of football and cricket and schoolboydom.'[1]

Having invented the adolescent, society has been faced with the problem of justifying his existence. This has been attempted in a variety of terms: social and economic (the need for a longer preparation for adulthood in a complex society), biological and evolutionary. Attainments, skills and attitudes appearing generally in young people before the theory supposed that they should, or, indeed, could, appear, had to be explained away.

Stanley Hall seemed to have found, at least to his own satisfaction, the ultimate justification in Nature, in the recapitulation of the history of the race. 'Along with the sense of the immense importance of further co-ordinating childhood and youth with the development of the race, has grown the conviction that only here can we hope to find true norms against the tendency to precocity in home, school, church, and civilization generally, and also to establish criteria by which both to diagnose and measure arrest and retardation in the individual and the race.'[2] This was a refinement of the views of Rousseau, to whom Hall acknowledges his debt.[3] The proper conduct of the adolescent could be inferred from the culture-epoch which he was, or should be, recapitulating: 'the adolescent is neo-atavistic, and in him the later acquisitions of the race slowly become prepotent. Development is less gradual and more saltatory, suggestive of some ancient period of storm and stress when old moorings were broken and a higher level attained.'

Unfortunately large numbers of adolescents—particularly, thought Hall, American adolescents (as Warden Sewell's informant would have agreed)—were failing to recapitulate the appropriate phase of racial history; they were, indeed, ignoring it altogether, leaping rather than growing into maturity, showing undue haste 'to know all and do all befitting man's estate before its time.' Perhaps, thought Hall, the fault lay in America which, as a new nation, was deficient in the appropriate historical sequences and had missed so many of the early phases of social

[1] See A. K. Boyd, *Radley College* (1948), quoted from a letter written in 1858.
[2] G. Stanley Hall, *Adolescence* (1905), vol. I, p. viii.
[3] Ibid., p. x.

evolution: they simply had not existed for American youth to recapitulate.

England has perhaps been more fortunate in her long history. She certainly appears to have been more effective in the social institutions she has fashioned to mould her adolescents of higher social rank. Whatever they are 'by nature', she has certainly *made* them approximate to the theoretical specifications with quite remarkable success. It is the great achievement of the English public school since the mid-nineteenth century that, while it has segregated the young from the major concerns of the adult world, it has conferred a status on its members which has, perhaps, proved adequate compensation. It has enabled an 'adjustment' to the social order relatively, though by no means wholly, free from friction, resentment and hostility.[1]

[1] See Betty Spinley, *The Deprived and the Privileged* (1953), for an inquiry into the social adjustment of public-school boys and girls in the mid-twentieth century.

Chapter Four

POPULATION CHANGES AND
THE STATUS OF THE YOUNG[1]

DURING the past two hundred years young people in
English society have moved through three broad status
phases: the first, from the 1780s to the 1860s, was a
period of high status, the second, from the 1860s to the 1910s,
a period of low; the third, from the 1920s up to the present time,
a high status phase. 'Young people' between the ages of 10 and
20, no longer young children, but not yet 'adults' chronologically,
socially or legally, have enjoyed a status which has varied with
population changes and economic opportunity. The best indices
of their status are probably the amount of marriage among them
and the extent of their independent income.

The status of the young has often been equated with the
extent to which they are protected from adult society. Such an
assessment shows increasing status throughout the nineteenth
century with every successive Factory and Education Act,
culminating in the last thirty years of the century, when the
regulation or prohibition of juvenile employment was extended
to a wider range of industry (including agriculture), when
compulsory education was introduced, and children were finally
protected from their parents by Mundella's 'Children's Charter'
of 1889 and the work of the N.S.P.C.C.

This is a proposition which calls for critical re-appraisal.
Protective measures are a two-edged device: while they may
signify concern for the welfare of the young, they also define
them as a separate, non-adult population, inhabiting a less than
adult world. The need for protection and distinctive treatment
underlines their less than adult status. The young were extensively

[1] This chapter is based on the author's 'Population Changes and the Status of the
Young in England since the Eighteenth Century', *Sociological Review* (1963), 11.

withheld from the economy and given compulsory schooling after 1870 when the economy no longer required their services on the scale that had prevailed over the previous century. The economy's diminished scope for juvenile labour was already evident in the sixties: not only was the demand decreasing, but it was shifting from the important, central industries like agriculture to employment more marginal to the economy, like domestic service. The statutes of 1870 and 1880 which introduced compulsory education were largely superfluous acts of rescue; they signalized for the young a displacement which had already occurred from a pivotal position in the nation's economic life.[1]

Demographic Influences

The rising status of the young in the Western world, measured by the protective provisions and welfare facilities increasingly at their disposal, has been attributed at least in part to their diminishing proportion of the total population. They are held to have acquired a scarcity-value.

'The present high status of childhood was not possible until a more economical rate of reproduction and the small-family system came generally to prevail.'[2] Their continuing scarcity is held to augur well for their position in the future: 'Many interesting consequences are likely to flow from the scarcity of children. They will probably be very much appreciated. Consideration will be given to them in building play space, guarding them from traffic, in providing nurseries for them in department stores.'[3] Similar arithmetic of population has been seen to underlie the rise of the child-centred family—particularly the *bourgeois* family —of Victorian France and England: 'La famille, réduite à la famille conjugale, s'est repliée sur les enfants qui constituent son noyau: c'est le triomphe du malthusianisme démographique.'[4] With the limitation of family size of which Malthus would have approved the child moved to a central, even a dominant, position in family life: 'Toute l'énergie du groupe est depensée pour la

[1] Cf. A. B. Hollingshead, op. cit., pp. 149–50: 'The establishment of high schools in the late nineteenth and early twentieth centuries may have been a response to the loss of economic functions of adolescents in American culture.'
[2] J. H. S. Bossard, *The Sociology of Child Development* (1954), p. 613.
[3] W. F. Ogburn and M. F. Nimkoff, *Handbook of Sociology* (1953), p. 337.
[4] Philippe Ariès, *L'Enfant et La Vie Familiale sous L'Ancien Régime* (1960), p. 317.

Population Changes and the Status of the Young

promotion des enfants, chacun en particulier, sans aucune ambition collective: les enfants, plutôt que la famille.'[1]

Even if we take protective legislation and the provision of educational and welfare services as the main criteria of the status of the young, this demographic explanation does not accord with the facts of nineteenth-century history. Protection and welfare came when the family was larger, and the proportion of young people in the population greater, than ever before or since. Charles Booth referred to the 'remarkable increase' in the number of children under 15 years of age to every 100 men aged 25 to 65, between 1851 and 1881: there were 179 in 1851, 181 in 1861, 185 in 1871, and 190 in 1881.[2] Dependent (unoccupied) children under the age of 15 years were increasing more rapidly than population: by 12·7 per cent compared with 11·9 per cent between 1851 and 1861, by 15·8 per cent compared with 13·1 per cent between 1861 and 1871, and by no less than 18·7 per cent compared with 14·5 per cent between 1871 and 1881. (In the latter decade, of course, the welfare provisions themselves were causing a greater number to be unoccupied.) The proportion of children (both dependent and occupied) under 15 years in the total population increased steadily: 35·4 per cent in 1851, 35·7 per cent in 1861, 36·1 per cent in 1871, and 36·6 per cent in 1881. By 1881 the young were never so abundant and never so protected. (Never before had they been so richly displayed—in Little Lord Fauntleroy outfits, sailor suits and Eton collars.) The declining birth rate came after extensive measures for child welfare, and not before—when the cost of welfare, particularly to the middle-class family, proved to be extremely onerous.[3]

The growing concern for the welfare of children is more satisfactorily related to the falling mortality rates at the end of the eighteenth century than to the falling birth rate at the end of the nineteenth.[4] Even the child-centred middle-class family

[1] Ibid., p. 457.
[2] Charles Booth, 'Occupations of the People of the United Kingdom 1801–1881', *Journal of the Statistical Society* (June 1886).
[3] See A. J. Banks, *Prosperity and Parenthood* (1954), ch. xi, 'The Cost of Children'.
[4] Cf. D. E. C. Eversley, *Social Theories of Fertility and the Malthusian Debate* (1959), p. 80. Bernard Shaw suggests that the power of children in the home declined as a consequence of the reduction of family size: 'Two adult parents, in spite of a home to keep and an income to earn' can still interfere to a disastrous extent with the rights and liberties of one child' (Preface to *Misalliance*, 1910).

to which Ariès refers can be seen at the earlier period: the seventeen children of the Edgeworth household were not too numerous to constitute the family's central concern, around whom domestic life was organized. (William Cobbett's farm is another good example of the child-centred, educative household, which was by no means uncommon at this time.)

Certainly the moralists and educationists of late-eighteenth-century England were unanimous that the (middle-class) child had never before been treated with such consideration and solicitude. 'The domestic discipline of our ancestors has been relaxed by the philosophy and softness of the age,' maintained Gibbon; 'and if my father remembered that he had trembled before a stern parent, it was only to adopt with his son an opposite mode of behaviour.'[1] Clara Reeve[2] and Mrs Sherwood[3] gave similar testimony; the Rev William Jones saw the importance given to the young as productive of 'a new generation of libertines, some of whom are such monsters of ignorance, insolence and boundless profligacy as never existed before in a Christian country.'[4] Both Hannah More and William Barrow attributed the changed standing of children to the pernicious influence of the French Revolution. The former regretted that 'not only sons but daughters have adopted something of that spirit of independence, and disdain of control, which characterizes the time . . . The rights of man have been discussed till we are sometimes wearied with the discussion. To these have been opposed, as the next stage in the progress of illumination, and with more presumption than prudence, the rights of women. It follows, according to the actual progression of human things, that the next influx of that irradiation which our enlighteners are pouring in upon us, will illuminate the world with grave descants on the rights of youth, the rights of children, the rights of babies.'[5] William Borrow was of the opinion that the new age's solicitude for the young begot all too often 'the character known amongst us by the appellation of a Jacobin or a Democratist.'[6]

[1] E. Gibbon, *Works* (vol. 1), *Autobiography*, p. 112.
[2] *Plans of Education* (1792), p. 39.
[3] S. Kelley (ed.), *Life of Mrs Sherwood* (1854), pp. 40 and 46.
[4] W. Jones, *Letters from a Tutor to his Pupil* (1775) (1821 ed.), p. 8.
[5] Hannah More, *Strictures on the Modern System of Female Education* (1801 ed.), 1, pp. 172-3.
[6] See W. Barrow, *Essay on Education* (1802).

A sensitive awareness of the nature and the needs of childhood, reflected in the literature of the age,[1] long preceded the spread of modern methods of birth control among the middle classes and the reduction of family size. Declining child mortality rates in the later eighteenth century made children worth taking seriously: when they were more likely to survive to manhood, there was more point in taking pains with their early training and education. The serious training for a career provided by apprenticeship had traditionally started only at the age of 14; Rousseau in the 1760s had recommended that systematic education was pointless before puberty. (The reasons he advanced were partly psychological, but he was fully aware of the likelihood that an early investment in education would be wasted.[2]) The considerable resources put into Infant and Preparatory schools after the 1820s make sense only in the light of declining mortality rates among their inmates.

The 'cruelty' with which children were treated in the eighteenth century owes much to the demographic circumstances of the age. Methods of hardening the young were devised in an attempt to combat the high rates of infant mortality. Severity was doubtless hallowed by puritan and stoic traditions; but the quasi-medical practice of hardening had been advocated by the physician, John Locke, and found ready acceptance in an age which discovered the principle of inoculation:[3] to be fortified against a disease one should first suffer its less virulent form or analogue.

Locke recommended fresh air, exercise, plain diet and 'not too warm or strait clothing' for the young; he also urged that 'the head and feet (must be) kept cold, and the feet used to cold water and exposed to wet.'[4] Rousseau went further, rebuking Locke for his moderation: he would have the young lie on damp grass,

[1] See W. Walsh, *The Use of Imagination: Educational Thought and the Literary Mind* (1959). Cf. J. Dunbar, *The Early Victorian Woman* (1953), p. 29.
[2] J. J. Rousseau, *Emile* (1762), Bk. IV. 'The way childhood is spent is no great matter . . . But it is not so in those early years when a youth really begins to live.'
[3] Although modern vaccination was not originated by Dr Jenner until 1799, inoculation against smallpox was introduced from Turkey in 1722 by Lady Mary Wortley Montagu with results which appear to have impressed the general public. Goldsmith in *She Stoops to Conquer* (1773) made Mrs Hardcastle declare: 'I vow, since inoculation began, there is no such thing to be seen as a plain woman' (Act 2). In fact it does not appear to have had much effect on rates of mortality: see G. Talbot Griffith, *Population Problems in the Age of Malthus* (1926), pp. 249–50.
[4] *Thoughts concerning Education*, sec. 30.

go without sleep, and sleep on the hardest of beds—'the best way to find no bed uncomfortable'. These views were propagated in the educational manuals of the day. George Chapman, for instance, maintained that children should be trained to 'bear fatigue and all the inclemencies of the weather', sleep on hard beds, be almost continuously in motion, go with wet feet, and be left in the dark so that it would have no terrors for them.[1]

There is no doubt that in the most enlightened and progressive households such advice was widely heeded. Edgeworth followed this advice in rearing his own children, Thomas Day carried out elaborate experiments to harden the orphans Lucretia and Sabrina to the point where one or the other would be worthy to become Mrs Day. (Neither responded satisfactorily. The lady whom he eventually married proved her fitness by tramping Hampstead Heath in the snow to cure her enfeebled constitution.)

Mrs Gaskell has told how her aunt subjected an adopted child to a process of hardening by tossing her in a blanket and appearing before her dressed up as a ghost.[2] Southey's sister was hardened out of existence. She was dipped every morning in a tub of the coldest well water. 'This was done', says Southey, 'from an old notion of strengthening her: the shock was dreadful, the poor child's horror of it every morning when taken out of bed was even more so; I cannot remember having seen it without horror; nor do I believe that among all the preposterous practices which false theories have produced there was ever a more cruel and perilous one than this.'[3]

In fact, the rise in the later eighteenth century of the practice of hardening for essentially medical reasons opens up a new age of hope and importance for the young: they were no longer treated with the comparative indifference and neglect which arose from a sense of helplessness in the face of inexorably high rates of infant mortality. They were not now abandoned to their fate, until their capacity to survive had been demonstrated.

It is probable that in the eighteenth century fewer than half the children born survived to manhood.[4] There is no evidence of

[1] George Chapman, *Treatise on Education* (1790), pp. 115 and 122.
[2] E. C. Gaskell, *Life of Charlotte Bronte* (1857), pp. 55–6.
[3] C. C. Southey (ed.), *Life and Correspondence of Robert Southey* (1949 ed.), vol. I, pp. 28–9.
[4] *Report of the Royal Commission on Population* (1949), p. 6.

marked differences between the social classes: children's stories, which had a wide circulation, written for upper- and middle-class children prepared parents and children for the latter's probable early death.[1] In these circumstances children were of little account before they reached puberty. Rousseau asked what was the point of a rigorous education 'which sacrifices the present to an uncertain future . . . and begins by making the child miserable, in order to prepare him for some far-off happiness which he may never enjoy?'[2] The basis of this advice to upper- and middle-class parents was the alleged fact that 'of all the children who are born, scarcely one half reach adolescence, and it is very likely that your pupil will not live to be a man.' (Even a century later Trollope's Dr Thorne would not have early education made exacting for similar reasons: 'Why struggle after future advantage at the expense of present pain, seeing that the results were so very doubtful?'[3])

In the later eighteenth century and throughout the nineteenth, child mortality rates declined. While the significance of the eighteenth-century decline for population growth may be disputed,[4] no leading demographer would deny that it occurred. The middle- and upper-classes could avail themselves more easily than the working classes of improved housing, sanitation and medical care;[5] the survival rate among their children up to 15 years of age was 83 per cent in 1871; in the population at large, while it was much improved on the rough estimate of 50 per cent a century earlier, it was still only 63 per cent.[6] It seems likely that the social-class differential had widened in the course of the nineteenth century. In 1830 79 per cent of the children of clergymen in the diocese of Canterbury survived their first 15 years, in 1871 85 per cent did so.[7]

[1] See James Janeway, *A Token for Children* (1671), Thomas White, *A Little Book for Little Children* (1702 ed.), Henry Jessey, *A Looking-Glass for Children* (1672), and James Whitaker, *Comfort for Parents* (1693).

[2] *Emile*, Bk. II.

[3] A. Trollope, *Dr Thorne* (1858), ch. 3.

[4] See H. J. Habakkuk, 'English Population in the Eighteenth Century', *The Economic History Review* (1953), 4, 2nd series.

[5] Cf. J. Hole, *Homes of the Working Classes* (1866), p. 17 for details of social-class differences in mortality in 1864.

[6] C. Ansell, *Statistics of Families* (1874). Ansell's inquiry was among 54,635 upper and professional class children. The figure for the general population is from the Carlisle Tables.

[7] Ibid.

There is no necessary correspondence between falling mortality rates among young people and the growth of suitable employment opportunities for them. There can be little doubt that by the 1870s middle-class children, by surviving in greater numbers, constituted a growing burden on their parents while they were growing up and an increasing problem to place in acceptable work when their education was completed. It is probable that a social-class differential in fertility existed much earlier in the century—Glass has computed negative correlation coefficients between fertility and status in twenty-eight London boroughs which were not notably smaller in 1851 than in 1911 or 1931;[1] nevertheless, it is from the seventies that the average size of the middle-class family began its steep decline. The birth-control movement was a symptom of the superabundance of the young in relation to family resources and to the needs of the economy. 'It may be possible to bring ten children into the world, if you only have to rear five, and, while one is "on the way", the last is in the grave, not in the nursery. But if the doctor preserves seven or eight of the ten, and other things remain equal, the burden may become intolerable.'[2] But other things did not even remain equal: it was unfortunate for the young that they were most abundant when the economy, whether at the level of professional or of manual employment, offered diminishing opportunities for youth and relative inexperience.

The Needs of the Economy

In the later eighteenth century and the first half of the nineteenth, parents valued children more highly as their chance of survival improved; employers valued them more highly as technological changes gave them a position of pivotal importance in new industries. As the traditional system of apprenticeship broke down because of its irrelevance in the eighteenth century, and the

[1] D. V. Glass, 'Fertility and Economic Status in London', *Eugenics Review* (1938), 30. But cf. D. Heron, *On the Relations of Fertility in Man to Social Status* (1906): 'the intensity of the fertility-status relationship doubled between the middle of the nineteenth century and the beginning of the twentieth.' T. H. C. Stevenson thought that if analysis could be pushed far enough back, 'a period of substantial equality between all classes might have been met with.' 'The Fertility of Various Social Classes', *Journal of the Royal Statistical Society* (1920).
[2] T. H. Marshall, 'The Population Problem during the Industrial Revolution', *Economic History: Economic Journal Supplement* (1929).

legal requirement to serve an apprenticeship to a trade was repealed in 1814, the young were liberated to find their true level of importance in the changing economy. Debased forms of 'apprenticeship'—particularly parish apprenticeship—within industry still often prevented the young worker from achieving his true economic wage and the social independence that went with it. But this form of exploitation, often by parents and relatives rather than by plant owners, became less common in the early decades of the nineteenth century. The new industries were heavily dependent on the skills and agility of the young.

Moreover, before the population aged in the later nineteenth and the twentieth centuries, there were greater opportunities for young people to secure top appointments: promotion was not blocked by a glut of older men. Jousselin has contrasted the opportunities which the young enjoyed in the later eighteenth and early nineteenth centuries with their frustrations today: 'Du fait du vieillissement de la population, la situation de jeunesse s'est profondément modifiée. Il leur est beaucoup plus difficile d'accéder aux postes de responsibilité et d'initiative. On ne connaît plus de generaux de 20 a 30 ans, ni de préfets ayant l'âge des gouverneurs de l'ancien régime.'[1]

In remote areas, away from large urban reservoirs of labour, young people were a particularly large proportion of the labour force in early-nineteenth-century factories, partly because the pauper apprentice was the most freely mobile economic unit. But even where labour was abundant and there was less need to employ parish apprentices, young people were often a high proportion of the employees. Forty-eight per cent of the 1,020 workpeople of M'Connel and Kennedy in Manchester in 1816 were under 18 years of age.[2]

The demand at this time was particularly for working-class youth; but middle-class youth—at least the males—were also needed as commerce expanded even more rapidly than industry and called for a great army of white-collar workers.[3] Only gradually, in the closing decades of the century, were

---

[1] Jean Jousselin, *Jeunesse Fait Social Méconnu* (Toulouse 1959), p. 8.
[2] T. S. Ashton, *The Industrial Revolution* (1948), p. 116.
[3] Commercial clerks increased by 61 per cent 1861–71 and by 88 per cent 1871–81 while all occupied males increased by 13 per cent and 32 per cent.

'accountants', for example, distinguished from 'book-keepers'—(and Upper Division civil servants from Lower Division[1])—and required to undertake prolonged education and training before receiving the economic rate for the work they did.[2]

In the new industries parents were often appendages to their children, heavily dependent on their earnings. When the farm labourer moved his family to the town, it was commonly for what his children could earn: his own employment might be as a porter, or in subsidiary work such as road-making, at a wage of 10 to 13 shillings a week; his child (and wife) could earn more on the power looms or in throstle-spinning.[3] As Mr Carey commented in Disraeli's *Sybil* (1845): 'Fathers and mothers goes for nothing. 'Tis the children gets the wages, and there it is.' The fathers of the poor families imported from Bedfordshire and Buckinghamshire were fit only for labourers. There must have been many a Devilsdust 'who had entered life so early that at 17 he combined the experience of manhood with the divine energy of youth'.

Apprenticeship and experience in traditional industries were a handicap in James Keir's chemical works at Tipton, founded in the 1780s;[4] Andrew Ure noted in 1836 that 'Mr Anthony Strutt, who conducts the chemical department of the great cotton factories at Belper and Milford . . . will employ no man who has learned his craft by regular apprenticeship.'[5] Samuel Oldknow's spinning mill at Mellor depended on youthful labour; subsidiary industries (lime-kilns, coal-mining, farming) had to be provided for redundant fathers;[6] at Styal the Gregs had to develop an industrial colony to provide employment for the adult dependants of their juvenile and female workers. What shocked middle-class commentators on factory life in mid-Victorian England as much as the alleged immorality was the independence of the young. In London girls of 14 working in the silk or

[1] *First Report of the Civil Service Inquiry Commission* (The Playfair) (1875) recommended an Upper Division recruited from the universities distinct from a Lower Division of routine clerks.
[2] Until the Census of 1891 accountants were not distinguished from book-keepers. In 1880 the Institute of Chartered Accountants, in 1885 the Society of Accountants and Auditors were founded.
[3] See N. J. Smelser, *Social Change in the Industrial Revolution* (1959), p. 185.
[4] W. H. B. Court, *The Rise of the Midland Industries* (1938), pp. 230–32.
[5] Andrew Ure, *Philosophy of Manufactures* (1861 ed.), p. 21.
[6] G. Unwin, *Samuel Oldknow and the Arkwrights* (1924), ch. XI.

trimming departments earned 8 or 10 shillings a week: 'if they had cause to be dissatisfied with the conduct of their parents, they would leave them.'[1] Similar independence was to be found in the Birmingham metal trades: 'The going from home and earning money at such a tender age (of seven or thereabouts) has—as might be expected—the effect of making the child early independent of its parents . . .'[2] The Factory Commissioners reported in 1842 that by the age of fourteen young people 'frequently pay for their own lodgings, board and clothing. They usually make their own contracts, and are in the proper sense of the word free agents.' (Even the Poor Law provisions of the Speenhamland System had a similar effect in the early decades of the century. As Mr Assistant Commissioner Stuart stated in the *Report* from the Commissioners on the Poor Laws (1834): 'Boys of 14, when they become entitled to receive parish relief on their own account, no longer make a common fund of their income with their parents, but buy their own loaf and bacon and devour it alone. Disgraceful quarrels arise within the family circle from mutual accusations of theft.'[3])

While factory legislation was at least a potential threat to the earnings and power of the young, the Act of 1833 extended their independence by destroying the vestigial authority of parents in the textile—particularly the spinning—mills. Virtually autonomous family units, under the headship of the father, had infiltrated intact into some of the textile factories: Andrew Ure[4] reported in the 1830s that 'Nearly the whole of the children of 14 years of age, and under, who are employed in cotton mills, belong to the mule-spinning department, and are, in forty-nine cases out of fifty, the immediate dependants, often the offspring or near relations of the spinner, being hired and dismissed at his option.' The spinner paid his piecers and scavengers from his own wages. (In the mines outside Northumberland and Durham the young worker in 1840 was often even more completely under his father's authority; in South Wales 'the collier boy is, to all intents and purposes, the property of his father (as to wages)

---

[1] Charles Bray, 'The Industrial Employment of Women', *Transactions of the National Association for the Promotion of Social Science* (1857).
[2] J. S. Wright, 'Employment of Women in Factories in Birmingham', *Transactions of the N.A.P.S.Sc.* (1857).
[3] Vol. 9, p. 54.
[4] Andrew Ure, op. cit., p. 290.

until he attains the age of 17 years, or marries.' Butties received 'apprentices' at the age of 9 for twelve years—a system likened by witnesses to the African slave trade.[1]) The early regulation of the employment of the young, and particularly their shortened and staggered hours of work, had the effect, along with technological change, of removing them from the control of the head of the family who developed a more specialized role which 'no longer implied co-operation with, training of, and authority over dependent family members.'[2]

The importance of the young to the economy is reflected in the high birth rate which was particularly bouyant in the later eighteenth and early-nineteenth centuries. This is not simply to say that children were begotten for the benefit of what they could earn whilst still children; in an expanding economy they were valued as a longer term proposition. Talbot Griffith rejected as 'scarcely tenable' the theory that the high birth rate of the period[3] was caused by the economic value of children,[4] but conceded that 'The feeling that the new industries would provide employment for the children at an early age and enable them possibly to help the family exchequer would tend, undoubtedly, to make parents contemplate a large family with equanimity and may have acted as a sort of encouragement to population without the more definite incentive implied in the theory that it was the value of children's work which led to the increase of the population.'[5] Marshall was more inclined to see significance for the birth rate in children's earnings: 'By 1831 the birth rate, measured in proportion to women aged 20–40, got back for the first time to the level of 1781 (this is a guess); by 1841 it had slumped far below it (this is a fact). Now it is only fair to older theories to point out how this fall by stages, slow at first and then rapid, reflects the history of child labour and the Poor Law.'[6] Glass,

[1] *First Report of the Commissioners (Mines)* (1842), pp. 40 ff.
[2] N. J. Smelser, op. cit., p. 265. For the administrative complexities which the educational clauses entailed see A. A. Fry 'Report of the Inspectors of Factories on the Effects of the Educational Provisions of the Factories' Act', *Journal of the Statistical Society* (1839).
[3] 34·4 births per 1,000 living in 1780, 35·4 1785–95; 34·2 1796–1806 cf. 31·1 in 1700, 27·5 in 1710 and 30·5 in 1720. See G. Talbot Griffith, op. cit., Table 5, p. 28.
[4] Ibid., p. 103.
[5] Ibid., p. 105. Talbot Griffith saw economic expansion as having a direct effect on the age of marriage and hence indirectly on the birth rate (p. 106).
[6] T. H. Marshall, loc. cit., p. 454.

on the other hand, found little or no connection between the employment of children aged 10 to 15 and fertility between 1851 and 1911 in the forty-three registered counties.[1] The value of children for their earnings *whilst still children* is doubtless an inadequate explanation of the changing birth rate; but the value of children more broadly conceived, as likely, in a bouyant economy, to constitute an insurance against misfortune in later life and old age, is an explanation not inconsistent with Arthur Young's argument that population is proportional to employment.[2]

Habakkuk has attributed the growth in population during the Industrial Revolution primarily to 'specifically economic changes', and in particular to 'an increase in the demand for labour', but has pointed out that the way in which this demand operated (whether directly on the birth rate or indirectly through the lower age of marriage) remains open to question.[3] The experience of Ireland, as Talbot Griffith realized, provides the key to this problem. It was an embarrassment to Griffith's argument that in relatively insanitary Ireland population increased between 1780 and 1840 at almost twice the rate experienced in England; inadequate statistics made it impossible for him to prove or disprove his contention that a declining rate of child mortality was the primary reason. On the other hand, the comparative lack of industrial development in Ireland seemed to nullify the argument that the primary reason was increased demand for labour.[4] This latter difficulty is overcome if we regard Ireland-with-England—or at least Ireland-with-Lancashire—as a single field of employment, as the Irish themselves clearly did. The relatively unskilled jobs available in the textile industry were particularly suited to Irish immigrants; and before 1819 movement into Lancashire was easy—easier than moving in from

[1] D. V. Glass, 'Changes in Fertility in England and Wales 1851 to 1931' in L. Hogben (ed.), *Political Arithmetic* (1938). 'Correlations between fertility and child labour yielded coefficients of $+0.489 \pm 0.116$ for 1851, $+0.291 \pm 0.140$ for 1871, and $+0.043 \pm 0.152$ for 1911. Of these coefficients only that for 1851 is significant.'
[2] Arthur Young, *Political Arithmetic* (1774). 'People scarce—labour dear. Would you give a premium for population, could you express it in better terms? The commodity wanted is scarce, and the price raised; what is that but saying that the value of *man* is raised? Away! my boys—get children, they are worth more than ever they were.'
[3] H. J. Habakkuk, loc. cit.
[4] G. Talbot Griffith, op. cit., p. 66.

elsewhere in England—since the Irish were regarded as having no place of 'settlement' and so could not be removed by the Poor Law authorities if they became a charge upon the rates. But these were not young children seeking employment. Undue concentration on the earnings of *young* children has bedevilled the question of the value of offspring. At this time in Ireland— and in England too—'a large family was regarded less as a strain upon resources than as the promise of comfort and material well being in middle and old age.'[1]

Children were of value even and perhaps particularly as they grew up into adult life and work, as an insurance against misfortune, against sickness and old age. They were not an entirely reliable insurance, particularly with increased geographical mobility and the dispersal of the family; their unreliability, at least in London, was commented on by Mayhew in the middle of the nineteenth century[2] and by Booth at the end. Booth was under the impression that this unreliability had become more marked in recent years: 'The great loss of the last twenty years is the weakening of the family ties between parents and children. Children don't look after their old people according to their means. The fault lies in the fact that the tie is broken early. As soon as a boy earns 10 shillings a week he can obtain board and lodging in some family other than his own, and he goes away because he has in this great liberty.'[3]

The importance of children was undermined in the later nineteenth century by the growth of alternative forms of insurance. Indeed, 'insurance' in a broad sense—whether paid-up premiums, private means or a working wife—has demographic significance as a substitute for children. Children seen as insurance help to explain the apparent paradox, discussed by Stevenson, that in the nineteenth century high mortality appeared to promote large families rather than vice versa. Many were born when comparatively few survived: additional births were necessary to effect replacements. This was particularly the case when there was no other form of insurance against misfortune: amongst miners, whose wives were excluded from employment after the

---

[1] K. H. Connell, 'Land and Population in Ireland 1780–1840', *The Economic History Review* (1949), 2nd series, 2.
[2] See Peter Quennell, *Mayhew's London* (1949), pp. 54 and 76.
[3] Charles Booth, *Life and Labour of the People in London* (Final Volume 1903), p. 43.

1840s, child mortality rates were high, but so was fertility. High child mortality rates were also experienced in the families of the textile workers, but fertility was low also; it is arguable that replacements were not so necessary when wives were commonly at work. The low fertility of couples of independent means had perplexed nineteenth-century demographers. Stevenson considered that their low fertility was the most remarkable case of all: 'In their case, presumably, those anxieties and difficulties which militate against fertility are at a minimum, but fertility is also at a minimum.'[1] Once the rates of infant mortality had fallen, it was safe to assume that even a small family would survive to carry on the family name and estate.

Children were of diminishing value to couples who were covered by insurance. The birth rate at the end of the nineteenth century slumped not only among the professional and middle classes, but among artisans and skilled mechanics, many of them among the infertile textile families, who in large numbers joined Friendly Societies such as the Oddfellows, Manchester Unity (1810), the Foresters (1834), the Rechabites, Salford Unity (1835), the Hearts of Oak (1842), and the National Deposit Friendly Society (1868). By 1872 the Friendly Societies probably had some four million members, compared with one million trade unionists —and the latter had sickness, employment, and sometimes superannuation schemes too.[2] The decline in claims for lying-in benefit by members of the Hearts of Oak gives some indication of their declining fertility: between 1881 and 1904 the proportion of claims to membership declined by 52 per cent.[3] It is likely that they had less need of this benefit precisely because they were members of a provident society.

By the last quarter of the nineteenth century the status of the young was being undermined as a consequence of their earlier importance. Their value had resulted in their super-abundance.

[1] T. H. C. Stevenson, 'The Fertility of Various Social Classes in England and Wales from the Middle of the Nineteenth Century to 1911', *Journal of the Royal Statistical Society* (1920), **83**.
[2] See P. H. J. Gosden, *The Friendly Societies of England 1815–1875* (1961). See also Charles Booth, *Life and Labour of the People in London* (1889), *1*, pp. 106–11. The Hearts of Oak charged a comparatively high subscription of 10 shillings a quarter; they provided £20 on a member's death, £10 on the death of a member's wife, sickness allowances beginning at 18 shillings a week, lying-in benefit of 30 shillings, and superannuation of 4 shillings a week.
[3] See Sidney Webb, *The Decline of the Birth Rate* (1907), pp. 6–7.

As Yule and Habakkuk have observed, the children who are produced in response to favourable economic circumstances may still be there when the circumstances have deteriorated: 'the present demand is met only by a delivery of the commodity some twenty years later; by that time the 'commodity' may not be required.'[1] Yule speaks of 'a very large and quite abnormal increase' in the labour force aged 20 to 55 years in the last twenty years of the century; as young workers the 'bulge' had entered the labour market in the late sixties and the seventies.[2] This increase was 'not produced by any present demands for labour, but in part by the "demand" of 1863–73 . . .': the birth rate in the sixties and seventies was as high as in the quarter-of-a-century after 1780.[3] Moreover, in the second half of the nineteenth century the survival rates among older children and adolescents improved much more rapidly than among children aged 0 to 4 years. While the annual mortality per thousand declined by 11·3 per cent among boys aged 0 to 4 years (from 71 to 63) between 1841–5 and 1891–1900, the decline among boys aged 5 to 9 declined by 53·2 per cent (from 9·2 to 4·3), and among boys aged 10 to 14 by 53·0 per cent (from 5·1 to 2·4).[4] Thus whilst adolescents were a better 'proposition', since they were more likely to live and so justify what was spent on their upbringing and education, the wastage among them was small at the very time that the economy had a diminishing need for their services.

This is the prelude to the introduction of compulsory education between 1870 and 1880. Not only was there a 'bulge' in young people, but advances in technology were in any case displacing the young worker. In some industries, too, extended factory legislation greatly diminished his value in the eyes of employers: the administrative complications raised by part-time schooling deterred mine-owners from employing boys under 12 after the Mines Act of 1860;[5] the Factory Acts Extension Act of 1867 and

[1] G. Udny Yule, 'On the Changes in Marriage- and Birth-Rates in England and Wales during the Past Half Century', *Journal of the Royal Statistical Society* (1906), **69**.
[2] While the population increased by 11·7 per cent 1881–91 the working population aged 20–55 increased by 14 per cent; the increases 1891–1901 were 12·2 per cent and 19 per cent respectively.
[3] 34·1 1851–60; 35·4 1871–80; cf. 29·9 1891–1900. See G. Talbot Griffith, op. cit., Table 5, p. 28.
[4] S. Peller, 'Mortality, Past and Future', *Population Studies* (1948), 1.
[5] 23 and 24 Vict. c. 151. See A. H. Robson, *The Education of Children in Industry in England 1833–1876* (1931), p. 159.

F

the Workshops Regulation Act of the same year had similar consequences in a wide range of industries including the metal trades, glass and tobacco manufacture, letterpress printing and bookbinding.[1] The textile industry, on the other hand, which had greatly reduced its child labour force after the Act of 1833, maintained a high proportion of juvenile workers after the Act of 1844 which simplified the administration of part-time work.[2] Agriculture also took the Gang Act of 1867 and the Agricultural Children Act of 1873 in its stride—chiefly by ignoring them.

Technical changes in many industries were in any case breaking the earlier dependence on juvenile labour: steam power in the lace[3] and pottery[4] industries was being substituted for children's energy and dexterity; the dramatic decline in the proportion of young people engaged in agriculture in the second half of the century has been similarly attributed in part to technical development: 'A new class connected with the application of science to agriculture has sprung into being . . .'[5] Young people were no longer central to the economy; they were moving ever more onto the periphery, into marginal and relatively trivial occupations: street-trading, fetching and carrying, and particularly indoor domestic service.

The decline in the proportion of young people (under the age of 15) had set in before the 'slight dose of compulsory education' introduced by the Education Act of 1870[6] and the more effective Education Acts of Sandon and Mundella in 1876 and 1880. In 1851 young people under 15 were 6·9 per cent of the occupied population; in 1861 workers of this age were 6·7 per cent of all occupied, in 1871 6·2 per cent, in 1881 they were 4·5 per cent.[7] The following table gives the percentage of workers under 15 years of age in selected industries between 1861 and 1881:

---

[1] A. H. Robson, op. cit., pp. 204–5.
[2] The Act of 1844 reduced the minimum age of employment from 9 to 8 and limited the daily hours of children to 6½ which could be worked either before or after the dinner hour.
[3] A. H. Robson, op. cit., p. 133.
[4] M. W. Thomas, *Young People in Industry* (1945), p. 85.
[5] Charles Booth, 'Occupations of the People of the United Kingdom 1801–81', *Journal of the Statistical Society* (June 1886).
[6] 'By 1876 50 per cent of the whole population was under compulsion, but in the boroughs the percentage was as high as 84.' See H. C. Barnard, *A Short History of English Education* (1947), p. 197.
[7] All calculations in this section are based on Charles Booth, loc. cit.

TABLE III

PERCENTAGE OF UNDER-15S IN SELECTED INDUSTRIES

	1861	*1871*	*1881*
Agriculture	7·6	7·2	5·5
Mining (males only)	11·9	9·5	5·7
Metal trades	7·9	5·5	3·1
Quarrying and brickmaking (males only)	7·3	5·9	3·8
Bricklayers and labourers (males only) ..	3·2	2·8	2·2
Textiles and dyeing..	15·4	15·7	12·2
Indoor domestic service	8·8	8·9	7·7

Perhaps the most remarkable decline in the proportion of employed young people was in the country's major industry, agriculture. This industry, of course, was experiencing considerable difficulties at this time and its manpower contracting; but while the total number employed in agriculture declined by 24 per cent between 1851 and 1881, the number of young people under 15 declined by no less than 40 per cent. Under-15s in agriculture were 21 per cent of all young workers in 1851, 13·7 per cent in 1881. An opposite trend is marked in the case of indoor domestic service: under-15s in this employment were 11·6 per cent of all young workers in 1851, 19·7 per cent in 1881. In spite of compulsory education, while the employed population increased by 38 per cent between 1851 and 1881, young people employed in indoor domestic service increased over the same period by 55 per cent.

But in spite of the growing numbers of young people still employed in certain industries, while the total number of employed people in England and Wales increased by 12·4 per cent between 1861 and 1871, the number of under-15s employed increased by only 2·5 per cent. This is not because a greater proportion was attending school. What alarmed investigators in the sixties, and provided powerful arguments in the campaign for compulsory education, was not only the apparent decline in the proportion of children attending school but a decline also in the proportion at work. The consequence was an increasing proportion of young people in the very margin of society, outcast and neglected. 'And what are these neglected children doing if they are not at school?' asked James McCosh, after reviewing the evidence relating to Manchester, in a paper to the National Association for the Promotion of Social Science in 1867. 'They are idling in the streets and wynds; tumbling about in the gutters; selling matches; running errands; working in tobacco shops, cared for by no man . . .'[1]

Inquiries conducted by the Manchester Statistical Society and by the Education Aid Society in the 1860s had produced disquieting statistics. With a decreasing importance to the nation's economy, the young had an exiguous existence in the interstices of adult society. In 1834 there had been in Manchester and Salford 967 day pupils at school for every 10,000 inhabitants; in 1861 there were only 908. The Manchester Statistical Society found in a survey conducted in 1865 that among the children aged 3 to 12 in their sample, over a half were neither at school nor at work. The Education Aid Society found in 1862 in widely separate districts of Manchester that in 2,896 families investigated, out of every fifteen children aged 3 to 12, one was at work, six were at school, but eight were neither at school nor at work.[2] (There were in these families a further 2,882 children over the age of 12: while 81·3 per cent of these were at work, and 1·5 per cent at school, 17·2 per cent were neither at school nor at work.) Compulsory education was a necessity by the 1870s not because children were at work, but because increasingly they were not.

The Age of Marriage

Between the 1780s and the 1860s young people, particularly the working-class young, were able to approximate to adult status because of their importance to the economy. Superfluous apprenticeship was an artifice which kept a diminishing proportion in unmerited subordination, particularly in the regions of most rapid social change;[3] in 1863, before the National

[1] James McCosh, 'On Compulsory Education', *Transactions of the National Association for the Promotion of Social Science* (1867).
[2] See E. Brotherton, 'The State of Popular Education', *Transactions of the National Association for the Promotion of Social Science* (1865). Also J. Hole, *Homes of the Working Classes* (1866).
[3] See *Report of the Schools Inquiry Commission* (1868), 9. 'In the West Riding, there is so great a demand for juvenile labour, that the custom of paying premiums to masters with apprentices is almost obsolete. Indeed, indentures of apprenticeship are far less common than they were. Boys are seldom bound to masters; they begin to receive wages almost immediately after they enter a shop. .' (pp. 222–3).

Association for the Promotion of Social Science, its remaining vestiges were roundly attacked as 'a species of slavery', 'incompatible with the free institutions of this country', which, 'unsuited to the present advanced state of society', 'should be discontinued as a worn-out vestige of the past . .' These were not strictures on 'parish apprenticeship', but on normal apprenticeship for which high premiums might be charged, which might require seven years' training for 'what might be acquired by a sharp lad in three or four.'[1] The early nineteenth century offered youth a dominant and not a subordinate economic role. The young, in their 'teens, could attain an independence which gave them virtually adult status, a situation reflected in, and further confirmed by, the tendency to early marriage.

The independence and early marriage of young industrial workers were severely disapproved of by (middle-class) social commentators and legislators. The resentment of the high status of the young (and of employed women) echoed through the parliamentary debates on the regulation of factory employment. Social workers were surprised that people who worked long hours under conditions which the middle classes would have found distasteful did not feel sorry for themselves. Fanny Herz found young women factory workers 'exceeding tenacious of their independence and jealous to a surprising degree of even the appearance of condescension or patronage in the conduct of those who would approach them with the kindest intentions . . .'[2] Lord Ashley, in the course of the debates on the Ten Hours Bill, wished to regulate the conditions whereby women were 'gradually acquiring all those privileges which are held to be the proper portion of the male sex' and which promoted a 'perversion as it were of nature which has the inevitable effect of introducing into families disorder, insubordination and conflict.'[3]

Early marriage, the reflection and confirmation of the high status of young industrial workers, was generally deplored. Factory work was condemned for the young not because wages

[1] George Hurst, 'On the System of Apprenticeship', *Transactions of the National Association for the Promotion of Social Science* (1863). See W. Lucas, *A Quaker Journal* (1934 ed.), I, p. 44, for an account of a pointlessly long, expensive and futile tutelage in the early nineteenth century even for the profession of chemist.
[2] Fanny Herz, 'Mechanics Institutes for Working Women', *Transactions of the National Association for the Promotion of Social Science* (1859).
[3] *Parliamentary Papers*, 3rd series, 73, col. 1096.

were low, but because they were high. 'From the same cause, namely high wages, very many early and improvident marriages take place.'[1] 'The Census returns of 1861', runs a typical lament of the period, 'show that mong the population of Bolton, 45 husbands and 172 wives were coupled at the immature age of "15 or under"; in Burnley there were 51 husbands and 147 wives; in Stockport 59 husbands and 179 wives in the same category.'[2]

This tendency to early marriage dated from the later eighteenth century and has been attributed to the breakdown of traditional apprenticeship with its requirement of celibacy, to changes on the organization of farming, particularly to the decline of the custom of labourers 'living in', to the higher earnings of the young, and, more doubtfully, to the system of poor-law allowances.[3] Because of the few hindrances to early marriage and the high birth rate of the period the later eighteenth century and the early nineteenth have been described as 'an almost, if not quite, unique epoch in the history of the human race.'[4]

These circumstances prevailed in Ireland equally with England; and the social history of Ireland illustrates even more vividly than the history of England the close connection between the status of the young and the amount of marriage among them. The contrast between the Ireland of the later eighteenth century which Arthur Young described in his *Tour of Ireland* (1780) and the Ireland which American anthropologists described in the 1930s[5] is between a country with independent youth and early marriage and a country with subordinate youth and remarkably belated marriage.

Arthur Young was impressed by the independence of young people and the early age at which they married. The reclamation of waste land and the subdivision of land were important economic circumstances behind these developments. 'There is

[1] R. Smith Baker, 'The Social Results of the Employment of Girls and Women in Factories and Workshops', *Transactions of the National Association for the Promotion of Social Science* (1868). Cf. Fanny Herz, loc. cit., 'Owing to the liberal wages they earn, many of our young factory women become their own mistresses at a very early age . . .'
[2] R. A. Arnold, 'The Cotton Famine', *Transactions* N.A.P.S.Sc. (1864).
[3] G. Talbot Griffith, op. cit., pp. 112–22.
[4] See A. M. Carr-Saunders, *Population* (1925), pp. 38–41.
[5] Conrad M. Arensberg and Solon T. Kimball, *Family and Community in Ireland* (1940).

no doubt at all that in the late-eighteenth and early-nineteenth centuries the Irish married while unusually young.'[1] But whereas in 1841 only 43 per cent of males aged 25 to 35 were unmarried, in 1926 the percentage was 72. In the meantime the economic circumstances that had made early marriage possible had dramatically changed; in particular the shift from tillage to livestock production after the Famine, and the virtual cessation of the subdivision of land after 1852. By the 1920s, while 45 per cent of English males aged 25 to 30 were unmarried, 39 per cent of American, and 49 per cent of Danish, 80 per cent of Irish males of this age were still single.[2]

Wherever social and economic institutions restrict the freedom of young people past puberty to marry, their social standing is depressed. The institutions may be as varied as protracted compulsory schooling, apprenticeship, exclusion from employment, the dowry, the bride-price, the monopoly of wives by elderly polygynists, or exchange-marriage. A bride-price or a dowry which is paid by parents enables the latter to regulate and impede the progress of youth towards adult status; exchange-marriage, whereby a man could marry only when his father supplied him with one of his daughters to give in exchange for a bride, was practiced by the Tiv of Nigeria until 1927 and effectively diminished the status of the young.[3]

Arensberg and Kimball have described how in County Clare in the 1930s farmers arranged their children's marriages with a keen eye to economic advantage. Marriage conferred status, and until marriage, whatever his chronological age, a man remained a 'boy'. 'Even at 45 or 50, if the old couple have not yet made over the farm, the countryman remains a "boy" in respect to farm work and in the rural vocabulary.' 'It goes without saying that the father exercises his control over the whole activity of the "boy". It is by no means confined to their work together.'[4] Groups of 'young' (i.e. unmarried) men, unlike the 'cuaird' of older men, discuss no serious adult concerns; their main activity together is gambling. They have been effectively reduced to a condition of social subordination and irresponsibility.

[1] K. H. Connell, loc. cit.
[2] C. M. Arensberg and S. T. Kimball, op. cit., pp. 103–4.
[3] M. Mead (ed.), *Cultural Patterns and Technical Change* (1953), pp. 114–43.
[4] C. M. Arensberg, S. T. Kimball, op. cit., p. 56.

The Position since 1870

The depressed status of youth between 1870 and 1914, already foreshadowed in the sixties in their increasing exclusion from the central concerns of the economy and signalized in the imposition of compulsory schooling in 1870, is further reflected in the rising average age of marriage. The proportion of married males and females between the ages of 15 and 24 rose from 13·1 per cent in 1851 to 16·6 per cent in 1861, reaching a peak of 17·4 per cent in 1871; thereafter the proportion declined to 16·0 per cent in 1881, 10·5 per cent in 1891, 11·0 per cent in 1901, and the nadir of 9·7 per cent in 1911.[1] Recovery thereafter was faltering in the twenties and thirties, marked from the period immediately preceding World War II: 12·7 per cent in 1921, 10·4 in 1931, 20·1 in 1947.

The diminished proportion of young people married after 1870 was particularly marked in the middle classes—a reduction of status particularly keen for middle-class girls who had as yet no compensation in widespread access to superior occupational statuses. As Hetty Widgett observed to Ann Veronica: 'They used to marry us off at seventeen. They don't marry us off now until high up in the twenties. And the age gets higher. We have to hang about in the interval. There's a great gulf opened, and nobody's got any plans what to do with us. So the world is choked with waste and waiting daughters.'[2] The average age of those professional men and gentlemen generally who married between 1840 and 1870 was 29·9 years, four-and-a-half years above the average for all classes of workmen.[3]

The recovery of youthful marriage in the forty years after 1911 was greater than the decline in the forty years before. The proportion of males ever-married aged 20 to 24 declined by 38·6 per cent between 1871 and 1911: from 23·3 to 14·3 per cent; between 1911 and 1951 it rose by 66·4 per cent, from 14·3 to 23·8 per cent.[4] The recovery among young women has been

[1] Calculated from *Papers of the Royal Commission on Population* (1950), 2, *Reports and Selected Papers of the Statistics Committee*, pp. 195–7.
[2] H. G. Wells, *Ann Veronica* (1909), ch. 2.
[3] C. Ansell, op. cit., p. 45.
[4] These calculations are based on data in J. Hajnal, 'Aspects of Recent Trends in Marriage in England and Wales', *Population Studies* (1947), 1, and the returns of the 1951 Census.

more striking: the rate of marriage among young women aged 20 to 24 fell by 30 per cent between 1871 and 1911, from 34·8 to 24·3 per cent of the age group; it rose by 100 per cent (from 24·3 to 48·2 per cent) between 1911 and 1951. (The increase in the rate among girls aged 15 to 19—266 per cent—is still more remarkable.)

Titmuss, drawing heavily on the work of Hajnal, has claimed that 'These increases in the amount or quantity of marriage—in the apparent popularity of the institution of marriage—are . . . quite remarkable. They are also quite unprecedented in the history of vital statistics over the last hundred years.'[1] This is misleading: to claim that 'the amount of marriage' began to increase after 1911 and that the institution of marriage was never so popular as in the last fifteen years would require that the proportion ever-married in the population-at-risk—all those over the age of 15—had risen. In fact, there has been remarkable little variation over the past century: 59·3 per cent in 1851, 64·3 per cent in 1871, 59·7 per cent in 1911, and 63·8 per cent in 1931. The proportion of spinsters in the age group 45 to 54 was 12·2 per cent in 1851, 12·1 per cent in 1871, 15·8 per cent in 1911, 16·4 per cent in 1931, and in 1951, at 15·1 per cent, almost as high as in 1911 and higher than at any time in late-Victorian and Edwardian England. What has recurred in the mid-twentieth century is the popularity of *youthful* marriage. It is a sensitive index of the changing status of the young.

The young have attained a new significance in the nation's economy since the thirties. It is true that they remain ever longer at school—although the really significant fact of educational history since 1944 is not the (belated) raising of the school leaving age to 15, but the refusal to raise it to 16. It is possible that in the 1960s, as in the 1870s, the young will pay the price of their importance and comparative abundance in the previous twenty years.[2] As the bulge moves on to the labour market, the school leaving age will in all likelihood be raised, as foreshadowed in the 'Crowther' Report, *15 to 18* (1959), and the grammar-

[1] R. Titmuss, 'The Family as a Social Institution', *The Family: Report of the British National Conference on Social Work* (1953).
[2] Sixteen-year-olds may increase by 31 per cent 1957-63, the age group 15-20 inclusive by 19 per cent. See *The Youth Service in England and Wales* (the 'Albermarle' Report) (1960), appendix 6, p. 129.

school Sixth Forms, the universities and other institutions of higher education still further expand.

Since the twenties, and more particularly since the mid-thirties, the young have had the advantage of being born into an economy in which technological change has brought about widespread upgrading of occupations, the diminution of the proportion of labouring jobs, and an increase in the amount of skilled employment. Georges Friedman has argued that this is not the case: from his broad survey of trends in Western society, he scorns the notion of an imminent 'technicians' Utopia'[1] and claims that, while in the industrially advanced nations the proportion of unskilled labourers has declined, the proportion of semi-skilled, fragmentary, repetitive and mechanized jobs has greatly increased. The French[2] and American[3] statistics which he produces appear to support this contention that since 1910 the proportion of routine, semi-skilled workers in industry has greatly increased, while the proportion of skilled has shown relatively little change. The English statistics supplied by the Census Returns do not fit this picture: with skilled workers two-and-a-half times more numerous than semi-skilled (1951),[4] Friedman is driven to deny the validity of the Registrar-General's data: 'These surprising figures, which may even be regarded as mistaken when compared with the corresponding ones in France or the United States, can only be explained by fundamental differences in the definition and titles given to different occupational categories, partly perhaps also by the traditional policy of British unions, which attempt to maintain the status, and as far as possible the wages, of skilled trades for occupations that have been down-graded by mechanization.' He has less difficulty with American statistics in showing that 'from 1940 on, the proportion of semi-skilled workers is greater than that of either the skilled or the unskilled. Semi-skilled workers now constitute the largest group among the manual workers of American industry.'[5]

There can be little doubt that Friedman's thesis, at least with

---

[1] Cf. P. F. Drucker, *The Practice of Management* (1955) for the argument that mass production and automation mean more highly skilled and trained employees.
[2] Georges Friedman, *The Anatomy of Work* (London 1961), p. 169.
[3] Ibid., pp. 182–3.
[4] Ibid., p. 172.
[5] Ibid., p. 176.

with regard to England, is wrong. Although Erich Fromm[1] and Paul Goodman[2] appear to lend some support to his picture of American employment, their concern is more with the psychological satisfaction of work today, rather than with the level of skill it involves. This, of course, is a quite different question: 'alienated work', socially pointless and trivial work, may require high and rising levels of skill; it may nevertheless fall below the expectations of people who have lived through an age which has seen a revolution of expectation. But when Goodman argues that the status of youth is depressed, and their growing up to adulthood made difficult, because 'there get to be fewer jobs that are necessary or unquestionably useful; that require energy and draw on some of one's best capacities; and that can be done keeping one's honour and dignity',[3] he is, at least in the middle of this portmanteau proposition, stating an argument which is open to statistical verification. (He is forced by his initial assumption to the interesting conclusion that early (middle-class) marriage is today a *substitute* for satisfactory employment.)

There can be little doubt that the entirely contrary view put forward by Talcott Parsons is nearer the truth: 'We feel confident that a careful analysis would reveal that in contemporary organizations not only larger absolute numbers, but larger proportions of those involved are carrying more complex decision-making responsibilities than was true fifty years ago.' 'Now, not only have most of the older unskilled "pick-and-shovel" type jobs been eliminated, but an increasing proportion of the "semi-skilled" machine-tending and assembly-line types of jobs have followed them.'[4] In England the Registrar-General's classification of occupations shows a diminution in the proportion of employed males in unskilled and semi-skilled categories (classes V and IV) between 1931 and 1951: with jobs at both dates categorized on the 1931 classification, the proportion in class V declined from 17·7

---

[1] E. Fromm, *The Sane Society* (London 1956). 'There is one factor, however, which could mitigate the alienation of work, and that is the skill required in its performance. But here, too, development moves in the direction of decreasing skill requirements . . .' (p. 294). 'To sum up, the vast majority of the population work as employees with little skill required, and with almost no chance to develop any particular talents . . .' (p. 295).
[2] Paul Goodman, *Growing Up Absurd* (London 1961).
[3] Ibid., p. 17.
[4] Talcott Parsons and Winston White, 'The Link between Character and Society', S. M. Lipset and Leo Lowenthal (eds.), *Culture and Social Character* (1961), pp. 110–11.

to 14·3 per cent, in class IV from 18·2 to 16·0 per cent; on the other hand, the proportion of skilled men (class III) rose from 48·8 to 52·6 per cent.

The expansion and qualitative upgrading of skilled work has meant for the young that during the past quarter of a century they have grown up into a world in which the chances of obtaining skilled employment were steadily increasing. Mark Abrams has estimated that since 1938 the real earnings of 'teenagers' (defined as young people aged 15 to 24) have increased far more rapidly than adult earnings, by some 50 per cent; and that discretionary spending has increased by 100 per cent.[1] Although only 5 per cent of total consumer expenditure is in the hands of this age group which constitutes 13 per cent of the population over 14 years of age,[2] adolescent poverty may be said to have ended.

Young people have been obliged to enter 'dead-end' jobs far less frequently than thirty years ago: in 1951 they constituted a far smaller proportion of workers in the less skilled occupations than in 1931. The proportion of the employed population under the age of 25 has, of course, declined, from 25 to 18 per cent; but the decline in the proportion employed, for instance, as messengers, roundsmen, bus and tram conductors and lorry drivers' mates has declined much more steeply: from 91 to 35 per cent, 44 to 22 per cent, 27 to 14 per cent, and 85 to 67 per cent respectively. Their decline among unskilled workers in miscellaneous trades was from 25 to 16 per cent.[3] The less skilled occupations have become top-heavy with older people.

In consequence, as Abrams has claimed, young people 'Nowadays . . . are increasingly spending their working hours in jobs that require adult, industrial and literary skills, and the capacity to work with adults more or less as equals . . . Thus, in their jobs too, quite apart from their earnings, they have, economically, come much closer to being adults and much further

[1] Mark Abrams, *The Teenage Consumer* (1959), p. 5.
[2] Mark Abrams, *Teenage Consumer Spending in 1959* (1961), p. 4.
[3] *General Report, Census 1951*, Table 63, pp. 136–7. Cf. developments in post-war European industry: younger workers are getting better pay than older men and the general effect has been 'to confer the financial benefit of technical change upon these younger men with formal qualifications'. See *Steel Workers and Technical Progress* (1959): O.E.E.C. Project No. 164, quoted J. B. Mays, *Education and the Urban Child* (1962), pp. 157–8.

from the subservient roles of the child.'[1] These gains are by no means secure; they have given youth an importance and undoubtedly created an economic climate which favoured their greater reproduction. These very circumstances threaten their position in the future.

[1] *The Teenage Consumer* (1959), p. 13.

Chapter Five

INTER-GENERATION
ATTITUDES[1]

IN 1962 the author made an investigation into inter-generation
attitudes today. The aim was to examine the attitudes towards
adults of adolescent boys and girls in the secondary schools of
two socially contrasted areas in the north Midlands, and the
attitudes of adults in the same areas towards 'teenagers'. Although
little in the way of systematic inquiry into the attitudes of representative samples of adults towards adolescents was known to the
author, it was expected that the survey might show generally
hostile, critical and negative attitudes, but that there might be
social-class, and perhaps sex, differences. After the research was
completed the work of Eppel[2] was published showing the very
guarded attitudes of a highly selected group of English adults
(London magistrates, probation officers and youth leaders)
towards the present generation of teenagers.

American social scientists like Riesman[3] and Mead[4] have
alleged 'peer-group solidarity', conformity and loyalty among
adolescents and the progressive rejection, after later childhood,
of parental standards, values, guidance and companionship.
Psychologists like Stanley Hall[5] and Jersild[6] have reported
empirical research which shows American children after the age
of 11 abandoning parents as models for their future careers and as
advisers when they are in difficulties.

[1] This chapter is based on the author's article, 'Inter-generation Attitudes', *British
Journal of Social and Clinical Psychology* (1963), **2**.
[2] M. and E. M. Eppel, 'Connotations of Morality. The Views of Some Adults on the
Standards and Behaviour of Adolescents', *British Journal of Sociology* (1962), **13**.
[3] D. Riesman, *The Lonely Crowd* (1950).
[4] M. Mead, 'Social Change and Cultural Surrogates', in C. Kluckhohn and H. A.
Murray (eds.), *Personality in Nature, Society and Culture* (1948).
[5] Stanley Hall, op. cit.
[6] A. T. Jersild, *The Psychology of Adolescence* (1957).

The wide currency of these ideas led the author to suppose, when he began his inquiry, that his adolescent subjects would show a far greater preference than younger children for the society of their coevals; that with advancing years they would make in an attitude test an increasing proportion of favourable and approving references to their coevals and a declining proportion to adults in general and parents in particular. Psychoanalytical theory and empirical studies like Liccione's[1] into harmony and tension in child-parent relationships suggested the probability that at or soon after puberty boys' attitudes to fathers and girls' attitudes to mothers would be particularly hostile and critical.

The need to check the truth of these views, and particularly their applicability to English society, whatever their validity might be in America, is ever more apparent as studies in England and France throw doubt on the simplicity of this thesis regarding the parent and peer-group relationships of adolescents. The work of Morris[2] in England has questioned the notion of peer-group solidarity, conformity and loyalty (perhaps particularly among the middle-class young). He found that the proportion of adolescents who felt that they should support their peers in certain situations of conflict with adult authority 'declined sharply with age'. (On the other hand, the proportion who thought they would, in fact, support their friends remained relatively constant.)

The French *bourgeois* family, according to Pitts,[3] still enfolds its adolescents more completely and securely than the American family: 'The peer group cannot expect the type of loyalty that the American or English (?) peer group may claim.' Ariès[4] offers a similar analysis: 'la famille moderne se retranche du monde, et oppose à la societé le groupe solitaire des parents et des enfants.' Even in America the loyalty to peer-group standards and conformity to peer-group behaviour are now being seriously questioned. Murphy[5] reported studies of 'cordiality' at an

[1] J. V. Liccione, 'The Changing Family Relationships of Adolescent Girls', *Journal of Abnormal and Social Psychology* (1955), 51.
[2] J. F. Morris, 'The Development of Adolescent Value-Judgments', *British Journal of Educational Psychology* (1958), 28.
[3] J. Pitts, 'The Family and Peer Groups' in N. W. Bell and E. F. Vogel (eds.), *An Introduction to the Family* (1960).
[4] P. Ariès, op. cit.
[5] G. Murphy, *Personality* (1947).

American boys' summer camp which suggested that high status was determined less by conformity than by self-sufficiency; Lucas and Horrocks,[1] in an attempt to isolate the psychological needs of adolescents, failed to distinguish a specific need for peer-group conformity; and Riley, Riley and Moore[2] have recently found American adolescents less 'other-directed' than they had supposed, perceiving the different expectations of parents and peers, and themselves preferring patterns of behaviour which fell somewhere in between.

The view that adolescents become increasingly critical of adults and transfer their approval to their coevals seemed to the author to merit further investigation. The inquiry was also designed to reveal qualitative as well as quantitative changes in attitude. In particular it was hoped to throw some light in an English setting on the view of Parsons and Bales[3] that in the modern nuclear family the role of the mother is 'expressive' and of the father 'task-oriented' and 'instrumental'.

Whether the subjects of this inquiry made this particular distinction or not, it was expected that the qualities ascribed to parents would change between later childhood and adolescence, and that the behaviour of mothers and fathers would be sharply distinguished. But the attitudes to parents which have been reported in America were not expected with any confidence. Bronson, Katten and Livson[4] concluded from a study of American family life that both sons and daughters perceived mothers more often than fathers as exercising strong authority in the home; Nimkoff[5] has argued that the parent who habitually exercises discipline will not be preferred to the parent who does not. The (probably) different authority structure of the English family made it seem likely that the subjects in the author's inquiry, while they might ascribe to mother an expressive and integrative role, would not see her as the main agency of family discipline,

---

[1] M. C. Lucas and J. E. Horrocks, 'An Experimental Approach to the Analysis of Adolescent Needs', *Child Development* (1960), 31.

[2] M. W. Riley, J. W. Riley and M. E. Moore, 'Adolescent Values and the Riesman Typology' in S. M. Lipset and L. Lowenthal, *Culture and Social Character* (1961).

[3] Talcott Parsons and R. F. Bales, *Family Socialization and Interaction Processes* (1956).

[4] C. W. Bronson, E. S. Katten and N. Livson, 'Patterns of Authority and Affection in Two Generations', *Journal of Abnormal and Social Psychology* (1959), 58.

[5] M. F. Nimkoff, 'The Child's Preference for Mother or Father', *American Sociological Review* (1942), 7.

or the object of such strong hostility as Liccione found in his studies of American adolescent girls.

Plan of Inquiry

This investigation was carried out in the schools and among the adult population of two socially contrasted areas of the Midlands which were chosen because of the contrast they presented, because they were of manageable size, and because the head teachers of the schools were interested in the project and co-operative.[1] One town which was chosen is in the north Midlands, has a population of 51,000 and is engaged in heavy industry, textiles and mining. The second area, 60 miles away, is a suburb-anized village 10 miles from a large city. The original agricultural village is now heavily overlaid with new and expensive owner-occupied houses: professional and businessmen live there and work in the nearby city. Professional and managerial families predominate and the total population of the village is now 1,800. Most of the children of secondary school age attend a new junior comprehensive school, still comparatively small, in its early stages of growth, which also serves other predominantly middle-class neighbourhoods on the city's outskirts.

Three questionnaires were used with a selected population of school children in the two areas: (1) asking for preferred companions in a variety of activities and situations, (2) a social distance scale, and (3) an open-ended sentence-completion test. The children were asked to indicate on a list who would be their preferred companions in ordinary leisure activities: 'If you were going on an outing one Saturday or in the holidays (for instance, to the pictures, to a football match, or for a picnic) and could take any two people with you, whom would you most like to take? Father, mother, some other grown-up person, another, a friend as old as you of the same sex, another, a friend as old as you of the opposite sex, another, a friend older than you of the same sex, another, a friend older than you of the opposite sex, another, a friend younger than you of the same sex, another, a friend younger than you of the opposite sex, another.'

[1] I am indebted to Miss Dorothy Wass for her assistance in administering and analysing the questionnaires.

In order to discover how choice of companions might be influenced by the difficulties involved in the situation envisaged, the questionnaire also asked for preferred associates in three situations of ascending order of difficulty: 'If you were having a party and could invite any five people, would you want all of them to be over 30 years of age, some of them, or none? If you were going on a long and difficult journey with five other people, would you wish them all to be over 30, some of them or none? If you were in a position of great danger and could get five people to come to your aid, would you want all five to be over 30, some of them, or none?'

Social distance scales were also devised to measure the 'social distance' between the generations. No previous attempt to use social distance scales for this purpose was known to the author, but it seemed reasonable to him to adapt methods employed by Bogardus[1] and reported by Banton[2] in measuring social distance between racial groups, and by Shaw[3] for measuring the social distance between children of the same race and age. The social distance scales in Banton, Bogardus and Shaw were inspected for items which might be rephrased to apply to different age groups: in Banton and Bogardus seven items indicating different degrees of social distance were used, in Shaw, five. Twenty statements which seemed to indicate varying degrees of social acceptance of other age groups were drawn up by the author. Although the 'intervals' between these statements was clear from inspection, it was decided to confirm this impression by asking twelve adult members of a university extra-mural class to sort these statements out on a 5-point scale ranging from complete social acceptance to extreme social rejection. From each of the five categories a statement was taken which had been unanimously assigned to it by members of the class.

Social distance scales were then constructed to show attitudes to adults (over 30), to old people (over 65), and to people of the subjects' own age. The following questionnaire was used, and others appropriately modified to apply to different age groups:

[1] E. S. Bogardus, 'The Measurement of Social Distance' in T. M. Newcomb and E. L. Hartley (eds.), *Readings in Social Psychology* (1947).
[2] See M. Banton, *White and Coloured* (1959).
[3] H. Shaw, 'Popular and Unpopular Children', *Educational Review* (1954), **6**.

Tick one statement with which you agree:

1. I should like to spend all my spare time with people of my own age and with no-one else.
2. I should like to spend a good deal of my spare time with people of my own age, but not all of it.
3. I don't mind people of my own age being around, but don't want much to do with them.
4. I don't mind having people of my own age around just once in a while.
5. I like it best when people of my own age aren't around at all.

In order to discover changing attitudes to their coevals, to adults in general, and to parents in particular, with increasing age, the adolescents in this inquiry were also given an open-ended, sentence-completion test. Both Riley and Morris forced responses to particular situations: the former presented subjects with personality 'vignettes', the latter with descriptions of problem situations in which there was conflict between the attitudes, values and behaviour of friends, on the one hand, and parents or other adult authorities, on the other. In the author's inquiry as free a response as possible was sought, although the problem of subsequent analysis was thereby made much more difficult. All the subjects were simply asked to complete in any way they liked twelve sentences for which openings were provided: 'Mothers are . . . Mothers can . . . Mothers should . . . Fathers are . . . Fathers can . . . Fathers should . . . Grown-ups are . . . Grown-ups can . . . Grown-ups should . . . Boys (or girls) of my age are . . . Boys (or girls) of my age can . . . Boys (or girls) of my age should . . .' The age, sex, and father's occupation (as the best single criterion of 'social class') were obtained for each child who completed a questionnaire. All questionnaires were completed anonymously.

A questionnaire was sent by post to a random sample of adults in the two selected areas. Every two-hundred-and-fiftieth person was selected from the electoral roll of Midland town, every tenth person from the electoral roll of suburbanized village. Again the intention was to permit the freest possible response. The Eppels inquired only among adults in positions of authority and asked for answers to four specific questions (with two subsidiaries); for instance, 'Do you think that the morals of young people today differ from those that applied when you were in your teens?' In the author's inquiry six brief sentence openings were provided and the respondents were asked to complete them in any way they wished which gave their true opinion of the general run of teenagers as they had experienced them. The six sentence-openings were: 'Teenage boys are . . . Teenage boys can . . . Teenage boys should . . . Teenage girls are . . . Teenage girls can . . . Teenage girls should . . .' The questionnaires were completed anonymously, but details of age, marital status, family composition, occupation or former occupation if retired (and husband's occupation in the case of married women) were asked for.

The sentence-completion schedule which had been prepared for the use of adolescents was filled in by 302 boys and girls aged 11 to 15 (inclusive) in two secondary schools in Midland town and by fifty-four boys and girls aged 11–13 years in the junior comprehensive school which serves suburbanized village. These numbers were obtained by taking a random sample of one-third from the registers of each year of each school. The choice-of-companions questionnaire was completed by 200 additional children aged 9 and 10 in two junior schools in Midland town and by a further 224 boys and girls in a third secondary school. The social distance scale was completed by seventy-two of the junior school children and by 133 of the 14- and 15-year-old boys and girls in the secondary schools. The children of Midland town were predominantly (77 per cent) from the homes of manual workers; only 46 per cent of the children in the comprehensive school were from families of this social-occupational level.

Age of Preferred Companions

Seven hundred and seventy-eight boys and girls between the age of 9 and 15 indicated the two persons on the prepared list whom they would most like to have with them on an outing to the pictures, a football match, or a picnic. The percentage of choices given to parents declined significantly with each year of age except between the age of 10 and 11. The percentages given to parents by boys and by girls were not significantly different except at age 13, when girls gave fewer choices than did boys

(2·1 per cent compared with 13·5[1]); and similarly at age 14 (4·1 per cent compared with 10·3[2]). By age 15 boys had fallen to the same low level of parent-preference as girls—2·5 per cent in both cases.

Fig. I. Percentage of Companionship Choices Given to Parents

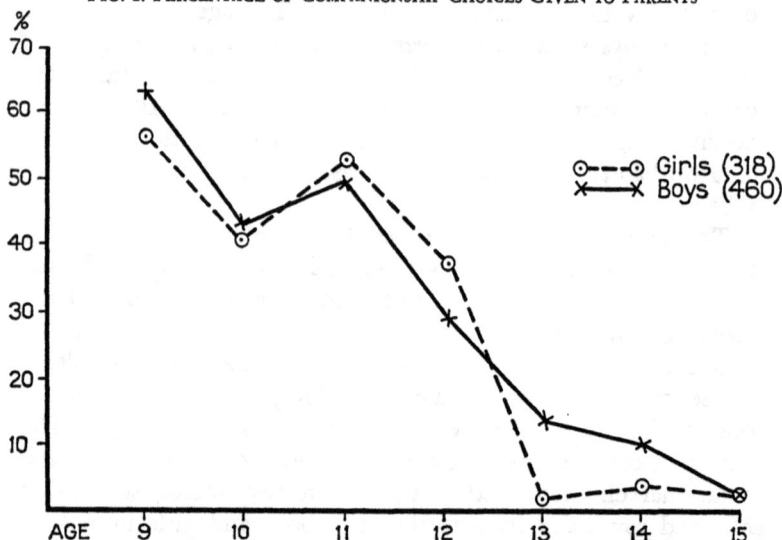

There was no tendency at any age for independence of parents to be correlated with level of intelligence or with social-class background. Intelligence scores (N.F.E.R. Group Verbal Tests) were obtained for two classes of boys aged 9 and 10: 60 per cent of the boys of below average intelligence gave at least one choice to their parents, only 47 per cent of the boys of above-average intelligence did so. The correlation with intelligence was not significant.[3] Twenty-eight girls of the same age showed no significant tendency to choose parents more often the lower their intelligence.[4] The correlation between intelligence and parent-preference among forty-four boys aged 14 and 15 was not significant.[5] Although some social psychologists have suggested that working-class adolescents are inclined to show greater

[1] P<0·01.
[2] P<0·01.
[3] $r_{bis} = 0·15$, S.E. 0·1.
[4] $r_{bis} = 0·264$, S.E. 0·1.
[5] $r_{bis} = -0·21$, S.E. 0·5.

independence of their parents than middle-class adolescents,[1] children from the homes of manual workers gave the same proportion of their choices to parents as children from the homes of non-manual workers.

There was a significant tendency among both boys and girls of all ages for preference for adult companionship to be correlated with the difficulty-level of the task involved. Seventy boys and girls aged 9 and 10, and 132 aged 14 and 15, were asked whom they would prefer to have with them in three situations of ascending order of difficulty. The distribution of their preferences is shown in the following table.

TABLE IV

PREFERENCE FOR ADULTS IN THREE SITUATIONS

Age: 9 and 10

	Boys (38)			Girls (32)		
	All	Some	None	All	Some	None
Party	—	20	18	1	22	9
Journey	3	32	3	4	26	2
Danger	11	26	1	20	12	—
	c = 0·54			c = 0·55		

Age: 14 and 15

	Boys (94)			Girls (38)		
	All	Some	None	All	Some	None
Party	—	29	65	—	8	30
Journey	3	67	24	—	28	10
Danger	35	56	3	10	25	3
	c = 0·59			c = 0·55		

The social distance scales, which were completed by 205 children, gave no support to a view which is commonly expressed, that the young are 'nearer to' the elderly than to the middle-aged; but showed that while young children (age 9 and 10) place no greater social distance between themselves and adults than they do between one another, young adolescents (age 14 and 15) hold adults at a significantly greater social distance than their coevals. Seventy per cent of the 9- and 10-year-old boys expressed a strong preference (by endorsing the first two statements on the social distance scale) for the society of over-thirties,

[1] See A. N. Oppenheim, 'Social Status and Clique formation among Grammar School Boys', *British Journal of Sociology* (1955), 4.

90 per cent for the society of their own age-group. This difference is not statistically significant.

Eighty-eight per cent of the 9- and 10-year-old girls expressed a strong preference both for over-thirties and for their own age-mates. At age 14 and 15, on the other hand, only 36·8 per cent of the ninety-five boys expressed a strong preference for over-thirties, 96·9 per cent for their coevals.[1] The corresponding figures for thirty-eight 14- and 15-year-old girls were 34·2 per cent and 94·7 per cent.[2] The proportion of boys and girls expressing a strong preference for the society of over-sixty-fives did not differ from the proportion expressing a strong preference for the society of over-thirties.

Adolescents' Self-Pictures

Three hundred and fifty-six boys and girls in three secondary schools completed the open-ended sentence-completion schedule. From the statements made about boys and girls of their own age it was possible to build up the self-picture which prevailed in each age-sex group. Thus in completing the sentence: 'Boys (or girls) of my age can . . .' defects were mentioned ('be spiteful'), physical competence ('climb trees', 'play hockey'), technical competence ('help', 'cook'), and social maturity ('go out with boys'). Boys and girls aged 11 to 13 (predominantly pre-pubescent) are compared under these four headings with boys and girls aged 14 and 15 (predominantly post-pubescent) in the following table.

TABLE V

ADOLESCENTS' SELF-PICTURES

(*Boys (or girls) of my age can . . .*)

	Defects	Physical competence	Technical competence	Social maturity
Boys (N 56) age 11–13	21·5%	41·1%	10·7%	26·8%
	(12)	(23)	(6)	(15)
Boys (N 116) age 14–15	39·6%	10·3%	7·8%	42·2%
	(46)	(12)	(9)	(49)
Diff.	$p<0·05$	$p<0·001$	NS	$p<0·05$
Girls (N 60) age 11–13	31·6%	8·3%	13·4%	46·6%
	(19)	(5)	(8)	(28)
Girls (N 102) age 14–15	32·3%	5·9%	2·9%	58·8%
	(33)	(6)	(3)	(60)
Diff.	NS.	NS.	$p<0·01$	NS.

[1] $\chi^2 = 77$, d.f. = 1, P<0·001.
[2] $\chi^2 = 30$, d.f. = 1, P<0·001.

The younger girls mentioned activities which denote social maturity more often than the younger boys.[1] Younger girls differ little from older girls in their over-all self-picture, except that they claim technical competence more often. The most striking contrast is between younger and older boys. The latter mention defects, but also claim social maturity, more often, and physical competence significantly less frequently.

In completing the sentence beginning: 'Boys (or girls) of my age should . . .' younger girls again differed little from older girls in the type and frequency of their responses; both expressed a particularly strong sense of personal responsibility. Younger boys differed markedly from older boys in their more frequent mention of physical skills and their less frequent references to social-personal responsibility. Statements could be classified into the five categories used in Table VI.

TABLE VI

BEHAVIOUR PRESCRIBED BY ADOLESCENTS FOR ADOLESCENTS
('*Boys (or girls) of my age should . . .*')

1 Respect for adults '*Consider parents' point of view*' etc.	2 Independence of adults '*Be able to stay out till 11 p.m.*', '*Be allowed more freedom*'	3 Friendliness to age-mates '*Mix together*', '*Go around together*'	4 Sense of responsibility '*Be sensible*', '*Act their age*'	5 Physical skills '*Do sport*', '*Keep fit*'
		Girls		
		(N 58, age 11–13)		
17·2% (10)	8·6% (5)	12·1% (7)	56·9% (33)	5·2% (3)
		(N 104, age 14–15)		
15·4% (16)	7·7% (8)	19·2% (20)	52·9% (55)	5·8% (6)
Diff. NS.	NS.	NS.	NS.	NS.
		Boys		
		(N 57, age 11–13)		
8·8% (3)	10·5% (6)	17·6% (10)	43·8% (25)	19·3% (11)
		(N 112, age 14–15)		
13·4% (15)	8·0% (9)	10·7% (12)	61·7% (69)	6·2% (7)
Diff. NS.	NS.	NS.	$p<0.05$	$p<0.01$

[1] C.R. = 2·64, P$<$0·01.

Attitude to Adults

In completing sentences which began: 'Mothers can . . . Fathers can . . .' the exercise of authority was mentioned ('can hit you if they like', 'can be too bossy'), but more frequently at all ages personal qualities unconnected with the exercise of authority ('can be generous', 'can get worried') and technical proficiency ('can mend things', 'can dig the garden'). The younger boys and girls were alike in the frequency with which their responses fell into these three categories; the older girls mentioned personal attributes of both fathers and mothers more often than boys of the same age, and technical proficiency less.

Neither the younger nor the older boys and girls in this inquiry appeared to see mothers and fathers in the contrasted 'expressive' and 'instrumental' roles postulated by Parsons: the younger children did not mention technical competence more often when referring to fathers than to mothers. In the older age groups, however, girls saw both mothers and fathers as predominantly 'expressive', boys saw both mothers and fathers as predominantly 'task-oriented' and 'instrumental'. There was no significant tendency at any age for either boys or girls to mention the exercise of authority by one parent more often than they mentioned its exercise by the other.

TABLE VII

ADOLESCENTS' PERCEPTIONS OF PARENTS
('*Mothers can . . . Fathers can . . .*')

	Mothers			Fathers		
	Exercise of authority	Personal attributes	Technical proficiency	Exercise of authority	Personal attributes	Technical proficiency
Boys (N 57)	15·8%	40·4%	43·8%	26·3%	35·3%	38·4%
age 11–13	(9)	(23)	(25)	(15)	(20)	(22)
Girls (N 59)	15·2%	52·6%	32·2%	23·6%	42·4%	34·0%
age 11–13	(9)	(31)	(19)	(14)	(25)	(20)
Boys (N 120)	15·0%	44·2%	40·8%	18·8%	45·4%	35·8%
age 14–15	(18)	(53)	(49)	(22)	(53)	(42)
Girls (N 106)	16·3%	59·0%	24·7%	17·0%	63·2%	19·8%
age 14–15	(17)	(62)	(26)	(18)	(67)	(21)
Diff.	NS.	$p<0.05$	$p<0.01$	NS.	$p<0.01$	$p<0.01$

The exercise of authority by parents and other adults was by no means invariably mentioned with disapproval. In completing the sentences beginning: 'Mothers/Fathers/Grown-ups

97

should . . .' reference to authority was made in approximately one-fifth of the statements. Younger boys made significantly more disapproving references than older boys, and older girls significantly more than older boys; but there was no difference between the younger boys and girls (see Table VIII).

TABLE VIII

MENTION OF AUTHORITY EXERCISED BY ADULTS,
MOTHERS AND FATHERS

	Approving (e.g. 'Grown-ups should not spoil their children', 'Mothers should learn their children manners', 'Fathers should make you do as you're told')	Disapproving ('Grown-ups should not boss us about', 'Mothers should not shout at us', 'Fathers should not hit us')
Girls		
14–15 yrs.	24	35
Boys		
14–15 yrs.	40	25
	$\chi^2 = 5 \cdot 4$, d.f. $= 1$, $p < 0 \cdot 05$	
Boys		
11–13 yrs.	17	27
Boys		
14–15 yrs.	40	25
	$\chi^2 = 5 \cdot 5$, d.f. $= 1$, $p < 0 \cdot 05$	
Girls		
11–13 yrs.	12	13
Boys		
11–13 yrs.	17	27
	Diff. NS.	

Although the social distance scale and the choice-of-companions questionnaire showed the expected increase in independence of adults with age, there was no corresponding increase in hostility and disapproval expressed in the sentences beginning: 'Grown-ups/Mothers/Fathers are . . .' One hundred and seventy-eight boys and 170 girls between the age of 11 and 15 (inclusive) completed these three sentences; all the sentences (and also the sentences beginning 'Boys (or girls) of my age are . . .') were classified 'favourable', 'intermediate', or 'unfavourable'. Thus 'Mothers are wonderful' was classified favourable, 'Fathers are big-headed/always at the pub' unfavourable; sentences which simply stated facts ('Mothers are grown-up') or a halfway attitude ('all right sometimes, not at others') were classified intermediate. Similarly with statements about their own age-sex group; statements such as: 'Boys of my age are bullies' were classified unfavourable, 'looking for jobs/still at school' intermediate, 'sensible/good pals' favourable.

Boys aged 15 made the lowest proportion of favourable statements (31 per cent) about fathers. (At age 14, 66·6 per cent of their statements were favourable.[1]) With the girls the lowest proportion of favourable statements about mothers (73·7 per cent) came a year earlier, at age 14. (At 15, 86·8 per cent of their statements were favourable.[2]) On the other hand, there was no corresponding increase in either boys' or girls' favourable statements about the parent of the opposite sex (nor was there any transfer of approval to their own age-sex group). (See Table IX).

TABLE IX

PERCENTAGE OF FAVOURABLE STATEMENTS ABOUT GROWN-UPS, MOTHERS, FATHERS, AND PEERS

	Grown-ups	Fathers	Mothers	Own Age-Sex
By boys				
11–13 yrs.				
N 57	40·3	51·0	70·0	42·1
14 yrs.				
N 63	49·2	66·6	77·7	49·2
15 yrs.				
N 58	38·0	31·0	72·4	38·0
By girls				
11–13 yrs.				
N 60	48·3	56·6	85·0	61·6
14 yrs.				
N 57	44·0	49·1	73·7	35·1
15 yrs.				
N 53	39·6	37·7	86·8	66·0

There was no social-class difference at any age in the proportion of favourable attitudes to their elders. In Midland town the social range was not great; in the suburban school it was wide enough to make a comparison possible. 53·3 per cent of the statements made about adults by boys from white-collar and supervisory homes were favourable, 53·8 per cent of the statements made by boys from the families of manual workers; 80 per cent of the statements made by the former about mothers were favourable, 92·3 per cent of those made by the latter; 60 per cent of the statements made by the former about fathers

[1] C.R. = 3·9, P<0·001.
 C.R. = 5·1, P<0·001.

were favourable, 77 per cent of the statements made by the latter. The differences between these percentages were not statistically significant. There was a similar measure of agreement between the statements made by the girls from the homes of white-collar and of manual workers.

Adults' Attitudes to Adolescents

The questionnaire which had been drawn up for adults was sent to 145 men and women in Midland town and to 125 in suburbanized village. 47 (32·4 per cent) were returned from the former, 24 by women and 23 by men. 22 of the women (91·6 per cent) were married, and all of the men; 15 of the women (62·5 per cent) and 17 of the men (73·9 per cent) were or had been parents of teenage children. The average age of the men was 53 years, of the women 50 years. 43 questionnaires were returned by the village (34·4 per cent). The 24 men, whose average age was 45 years, were all married and 46 per cent were or had been parents of teenage children; 18 of the 19 women who replied (average age 44 years) were married and 15 (79 per cent) had teenage children.

The sample drawn from Midland town was slightly biased towards the higher occupational grades, and more pronounced in its bias towards the higher age ranges. (Since the village is a civil parish within a rural district, it was not possible to obtain data from the Census relating to the age and occupations of the population.) Married women were assigned to the same social class as their husbands. Whereas 25·5 per cent of the sample were in Classes I and II, 51 per cent in Class III, and 23·5 per cent in Classes IV and V, the corresponding percentages for males over the age of 15 were 12·5 per cent, 54·8 per cent and 32·7 per cent.[1]

The sample was significantly older than the population of origin: 2·1 per cent were aged 20 to 29, 31·9 per cent 30 to 44, and 66 per cent over 45. The corresponding proportions for the adult population were 19·6 per cent, 33·6 per cent, and 46·8 per cent.[2]

The analysis of the questionnaires showed no difference in type of response between the two areas when social class was held constant. The two samples are therefore combined, giving

[1] $\chi^2 = 7·6$, d.f. = 2, P<0·05.
[2] $\chi^2 = 11·04$, d.f. = 2, P<0·01.

45 people (50 per cent) in Classes I and II, 29 (32·2 per cent) in Class III, and 16 (17·8 per cent) in Classes IV and V.

The completed sentences beginning: 'Teenage boys are . . .' and 'Teenage girls are . . .' were placed in three categories: (1) wholly or mainly critical and disapproving, (2) intermediate or neutral and (3) wholly or mainly favourable and approving. The following are examples of statements in the first category: 'Teenage girls are conceited and selfish/excessively frivolous/far too impressionable/guilty of widespread immorality: it is horrifying how many girls have had intercourse in their teens, even as infants.' 'Teenage boys are arrogant and disrespectful/discourteous and pig-headed/sexually inclined and pleasure-seeking/given to theft, idleness and disobedience—much more so than in my own youth.' The following statements were placed in the third category: 'Teenage girls are more intelligent than in former generations/as sweet as they were fifty years ago/attractive/more intelligent than boys.' 'Teenage boys are bright and clever/ sounder mentally and physically than ever before/idealistic and full of energy/more sensible than girls/mostly well dressed and well behaved.' Intermediate statements were: '. . . willing workers but foolish with money/all right provided they have proper guidance/very difficult to understand/confident but materially minded/pleasant but too advanced for their age'.

There was no tendency among the 90 men and women who returned the questionnaires for attitudes to teenagers to vary significantly with age, sex or family composition. No social-class differences were apparent in attitudes to teenage girls, but men and women in Social Classes I and II were significantly less favourable in their attitude to teenage boys than were men and women in Social Classes III–V. Only 7 out of 48 men and women in Classes I and II (14·6 per cent) expressed a wholly or mainly favourable attitude to boys, but 16 out of 42 men and women in Classes III–V (38·1 per cent) did so.[1]

The 540 sentences which had been completed were examined for dominant themes. Characteristics were most frequently ascribed to teenagers in four areas of behaviour: (1) rate of social-personal development: precocity, (2) tendency to be easily influenced and led, (3) appearance, (4) attitude to work. Teenage behaviour was most frequently prescribed in three areas: (1)

[1] C.R. = 2·5, $P < 0.02 > 0.01$.

helping in the home (most frequently for girls), (2) more training in housecraft (girls), (3) submission to firmer discipline (boys and girls). (See Table X.)

TABLE X
NINETY ADULTS' PERCEPTIONS OF ADOLESCENTS

	Boys	Girls
Ascribed behaviour		
Precocious (*'forward'*, *'too sophisticated'* etc.)	Nil	34·4% (31)
Badly dressed (*'slovenly'*, *'over-dressed'* etc.)	2·2% (2)	13·3% (12)
Easily led and influenced (*'sheep-like'* etc.)	7·7% (7)	15·5% (14)
Lazy (*'workshy'*, *'feckless'* etc.)	33·3% (30)	10·0% (9)
Prescribed behaviour		
Should help in or about the house	3·3% (3)	12·2% (11)
Should have more discipline	23·3% (21)	15·5% (14)
Should have more training in housecraft	Nil	17·7% (16)

No social-class differences were discernible in the distribution of these statements. Thus both men and women at all social levels made disapproving allegations of girls' sophistication, desire to appear older than their years and generally precocious development. Equally stern references were made at all social levels and ages to the teenager's need for more discipline: 'Teenage girls should be given far more discipline, should be in by 9 o'clock, should have less money, and a sound thrashing for screaming at fools like Elvis Presley' (31-year-old lathe-turner). 'Teenage boys should have far more attention paid to the formation of their characters. Very firm handling of the large numbers of hooligans and gangsters roaming our country would stop their atrocious assaults on defenceless and elderly people' (80-year-old retired Brigadier).

The adults in this survey were far more hostile and critical in their attitudes to adolescents than were adolescents to adults:

TABLE XI
ADOLESCENTS' ATTITUDES TO ADULTS, AND
ADULTS' ATTITUDES TO ADOLESCENTS

180 statements by 90 adults
'Teenage boys are . . .', 'Teenage girls are . . .'

Wholly or mainly favourable	Intermediate	Wholly or mainly critical
23·9% (43)	9·5% (17)	66·6% (120)

231 statements by boys and girls aged 14–15
'Grown-ups are . . .'

| 42·8% (99) | 20·9% (48) | 36·3% (84) |

$$\chi^2 = 37·3, \text{ d.f.} = 2, p < 0·001$$

Some Implications

Our prediction that between later childhood and early adolescence boys and girls would increasingly prefer their coevals to their parents as leisure-time companions was, not surprisingly, supported by the inquiry; but their movement towards independence of parents was less uniform than had been expected. In the case of both boys and girls a higher percentage chose parents rather than peers at age 11 than at age 10. No light is thrown by this study on the reasons for this. It is possible that the uncertainties which are associated with the onset of puberty, or even the disturbances associated with transfer from junior to secondary schools, are in some measure responsible.

In the light of previous research in this field, perhaps the most interesting results are those relating to changes in favourable and unfavourable attitudes towards parents. The stronger disapproval of adult authority expressed by pre-pubescent boys and by post-pubescent girls than by any other age-sex group is probably susceptible to a social-cultural explanation. The younger boys, turbulent even in their own eyes, and the older girls, 'forward' at least in the eyes of adults, probably feel the constraints of adult authority more than other children, and have greater reason to refer to it with disfavour.

The peak period of hostility towards the parent of the same sex, 15 years for boys and 14 for girls, is broadly in line with Liccione's findings in America and confirmed our original expectation. On the other hand, at no age did either boys or girls indicate the high degree of hostility to mothers that Liccione found among American adolescent girls. A far greater proportion of hostile and critical statements was made by both boys and girls of all ages about fathers than about mothers. Although 14-year-old girls made fewer favourable comments about mothers than older or younger girls, no less than 73·7 per cent of their comments were still favourable. Liccione argued that his findings could be adequately interpreted in the light of social-cultural theories as well as psychoanalytical frames of reference. The American mother probably pays the price for taking a dominant, disciplinary role within the family; English mothers are perhaps at an advantage in not enjoying a similar distinction.

This inquiry serves to underline the dangers of transposing

American research on the family to English society. We must do our own research. In the light of American work we supposed at the outset that boys and girls would sharply differentiate between the roles of father and mother. Pre-pubescent boys and girls appeared to make little distinction; neither did adolescent boys and girls, but by now their viewpoints had diverged. It is likely that both mothers and fathers behave similarly to their adolescent boys, and similarly again to their adolescent girls. The differences are between children of different sex, rather than between mother and father.

If there are dangers in transposing American work on the family to England, there are still greater dangers in transposing American work on the adolescent peer group. We began with the expectation that adolescents would show increasing hostility towards parents and increasing approval of their peers. There was little support in this inquiry for the often alleged 'solidarity' among adolescent males. Their approving statements about their peers were no more frequent than their approving statements about adults in general, less frequent than their approving statements about mothers, and up the age of 15 less frequent than their approving statements about fathers. They were less frequent than girls' approving statements about their own age-sex group. It is possible that the very intensity of adolescent male peer-group association is a cause of friction and hostility among them.

Our prediction that adults would more commonly express disapproval of adolescents than adolescents would express disapproval of adults was fully supported by the inquiry. Young adolescents showed themselves better disposed towards adults than adults were disposed towards them. The upper age limit of the adolescents who completed the questionnaires was, however, 15–16 years; whereas the adults were making statements about the whole range of 'teenagers'. It is possible that older adolescents are more critical of adults; although psychoanalytical theory would lead us to expect that the peak period of hostility, at any rate to parents, would be passed soon after puberty. The social circumstances of older adolescents, their greater social and economic independence and their increasing involvement in the affairs of adult life, might also lead us to suppose that they would be less rather than more hostile towards their elders.

The picture which adults had of teenagers was widely different

from the picture that adolescents had of themselves. The adults'
picture was overwhelmingly negative, with scarcely any reference
to teenagers' increasing social and technical competence. The
Eppels found that the 135 responsible adults in positions of
authority who replied to their inquiry were often unwilling to
make general statements in reply to the questions they were
asked; thus when they gave their views on the morals of young
people today compared with the morals of adolescents in their
own youth, 56 per cent 'withheld judgement'. But 29 per cent
were generally disapproving in their remarks, and only 15 per
cent appear to have been generally approving. This proportion
of approving statements is not dissimilar in magnitude to the
proportion in the present inquiry (24 per cent)—although it
refers to only one aspect of adolescent behviour, moral conduct.
One positive quality which the responsible adults saw in young
people today was frankness and intellectual honesty, which was
mentioned with approval by 22 per cent of the sample.

Although in some respects this study suggests important
differences from American conditions, it is in line with those
American investigations which have shown adolescents belittled by their elders, regarded as a separate, inferior, and even
threatening population, exposed to contradictory expectations
and demands from the general body of adults, and consigned, as
Hollingshead[1] has said, to 'an ill-defined no-man's land that lies
between the protected dependency of childhood, where the
parent is dominant, and the independent world of the adult,
where the person is relatively free from parental controls'.

[1] Op. cit.

Chapter Six

ROLE-CONFLICT IN
ADOLESCENCE

The Paradox of the Grammar School

THE grammar school ensures for most of those who pass successfully through it a relatively high social status in contemporary Britain. It exacts a formidable price for this service. Although it carries high prestige and has the confidence of the majority of parents at all social levels, it systematically humiliates its pupils, reduces their self-esteem, promotes uncertainties, ambiguities and conflicts in social relationships, a negative—even a despairing—outlook on life and society.

This is the classic prescription for the production of an experimental and deviant minority. Experiment and deviation have not in fact been remarkable among ex-grammar school pupils, particularly since the end of World War II, partly because the social and economic rewards which soon follow their chastening experiences have been, if not spectacular, at least adequate. Young professional men and women have never been so comfortable so early. But for many it would seem that the very capacity for vigorous deviation, or response of any sort, has been effectively paralyzed by their schools. Drilled in received opinions, carefully memorizing the steps which demonstrate established truths, the grammar-school boy only too often, as Hoggart suggests, loses 'spontaneity so as to acquire examination-passing reliability. He can snap his fingers at no-one and nothing; he seems to make an adequate, reliable, and unjoyous kind of clerk.'[1]

This condition is perhaps more often the fate of the less able, the border-line admissions. The potential irreverance and social inventiveness of the more gifted are effectively nullified by their

[1] R. Hoggart, *The Uses of Literacy* (Pelican Books 1962), p. 298.

subsequent social rewards. Jackson and Marsden have given us a depressing account of the orthodoxy of ex-sixth-form boys and girls from working-class homes who left their northern grammar schools in the nineteen-fifties. For the most part they were established in professional employment (many of them, as grammar-school teachers, already perpetuating their kind): 'Today, most of these eighty-eight children have developed into stable, often rigidly orthodox citizens, who wish to preserve a hierarchical society and all its institutions as they now stand.'[1]

It is arguable that such conservatism is a product of 'social mobility', rather than the outcome of experiences at school and at work in themselves. Perhaps these are characteristics only of *working-class* boys who have been through the grammar schools, symptoms of their anxieties and insecurities in a new social milieu. But there is no evidence that children who come from middle-class homes turn out to be more adventurous, more inclined to challenge established social patterns.[2] Indeed, the tiny handful of rebels who have graduated from the grammar schools into literary pursuits, the allegedly angry dramatists and novelists of the fifties, have been predominantly of working-class or lower-middle-class origin. There is no necessary relationship between social mobility on the one hand, and 'anomie', social rigidity and prejudice, on the other. American research has shown that 'low stationaries' may be far more reactionary than upwardly mobiles, who are not necessarily more or less interested in change and social innovation than 'high stationaries': 'mobility as a variable is weaker in its effects as a differentiator of attitudes than is status alone.'[3]

The experience of social mobility is probably irrelevant. A vaguely dispirited outlook yet a dogmatic support for the prevailing social order is likely to be found in any population, whatever its origins, which has endured a prolonged and frustrating apprenticeship but has finally secured the promised rewards. If the rewards were not in the end forthcoming—as they tended not to be in the economically depressed Europe of the thirties—the potential deviance could become explosively actual, providing

[1] B. Jackson and D. Marsden, *Education and the Working Class* (1962), p. 192.
[2] The small group of middle-class subjects in Jackson and Marsden's study were no less reactionary than the rest: op. cit., pp. 15-43.
[3] M. M. Tumin and R. C. Collins, 'Status, Mobility and Anomie: A Study in Readiness for Desegregation', *British Journal of Sociology* (1959), 10.

the motive force for revolutionary youth movements, widespread experimentation among a thwarted intelligenzia in daring social and political forms.

The effectiveness of the orthodox grammar school in promoting severe conflicts in its pupils is not seriously in doubt. But it has commonly been supposed that it is only the working-class child who experiences these difficulties at school: he has entered an alien world and is torn between the standards of school and home. Willmott and Young have reported the experiences of the girls of Bethnal Green who attended pre-war grammar schools. They were increasingly isolated from their neighbourhood friends and from their parents; yet at school they were aware of the social distinction between themselves and girls who travelled up from suburbs such as Ilford and Woodford. 'When they came home in the afternoon they were supposed to do homework instead of rushing into the street to play. They became different, lonely, "sort of reserved", regarded as "someone apart". "Oh, look at her," the other girls shouted after one of them. The uniform was a special trial—a mark of superior status detested because it made them feel inferior.'[1]

Hoggart bears similar testimony to the conflicts of the scholarship boy: 'For such a boy is between two worlds of school and home; and they meet at few points. Once at the grammar school, he quickly learns to make use of a pair of different accents, perhaps even two different apparent characters and differing standards of value.'[2] The assumption in all this is that the middle-class child finds in the grammar school an extension of his home, support for the values which prevail there, and a merciful escape from the conflict of living in two worlds.

But the evidence is that the grammar school generously and impartially inspires conflicts in its inmates without regard for differences in social background. It is true that there are some signs in empirical research that working-class children at the grammar school tend to retain values which are, perhaps, more common among working-class than middle-class people—boys are inclined to say, for instance, that they prefer friends who are good at sport rather than scholastic work, who enjoy a good

---

[1] Michael Young and Peter Willmott, *Family and Kinship in East London* (Pelican Books 1962), p. 176.
[2] R. Hoggart, op. cit., p. 296.

fight rather than thinking fighting silly, and who are interested in
girls and actually have girl friends.[1] But there is no evidence that
these persistent values influence their friendships or, within the
school, make them a race apart. (Indeed, in 'open-ended' statements by grammar-school boys about the characteristics of a
good friend social-class differences in value have not appeared at
all.) Oppenheim found in four boys' grammar schools no tendency
for friendship groups to form along social-class lines.[2] The
tensions which exist in the grammar school are doubtfully related
to social-class background and differences. Conflict is not the
monopoly of any single social-class group: it seems more likely
that it arises from the way in which the grammar school tends to
treat all its pupils. The grammar school afflicts all, with majestic
impartiality.

Eva Bene found no social-class differences in the 'affects,
dispositions, sentiments and feelings' of the boys she investigated
in four London grammar schools.[3] Using a sentence-completion
projective technique to investigate the attitudes and outlook of
618 boys aged 13 to 14 in four secondary modern and four
grammar schools, she found the pupils of the latter, regardless of
social background, more negative in their attitudes to others, to
life, and to themselves. They were more negative in their feelings
to school, to games, to siblings, to girls and to the world at large;
they were more critical of the manners and behaviour of children
and people generally, more inclined to see their parents and
teachers as hostile towards them.

Bene reflected on the results of her inquiry: 'After comparing
the environment in which the average grammar-school boy
spends his life with that of the average boy who attends a
secondary modern school, many would judge the environment
of the grammar-school boy to be superior. The parents of
grammar-school boys are on the whole better educated and more
intelligent, and they belong to a higher social class; grammar

[1] See A. N. Oppenheim, 'Social Status and Clique Formation among Grammar
School Boys', *British Journal of Sociology* (1955), 4. These differences emerged in
questionnaires which forced a choice between supposedly middle-class and supposedly working-class attributes in friends.
[2] A. N. Oppenheim, loc. cit.
[3] Eva Bene, 'The Objective Use of a Projective Technique, Illustrated by a Study of
the Differences in Attitudes between Pupils of Grammar Schools and of Secondary
Modern Schools', *British Journal of Educational Psychology* (1957), 27.

schools carry more prestige and give better education and better opportunities for future success than do secondary modern schools. However, actual comparison between the emotional attitudes expressed in sentence-completion responses of grammar-school and of modern-school boys indicates that it is the grammar-school boys who feel the more resentment towards their environment.' The pressures and high demands which grammar-school teachers make upon their pupils regarding academic achievement and standards of behaviour—and perhaps, too, their more generally authoritarian attitudes—can be expected to lead to a greater measure of frustration with consequent hostility and negative feelings. This may be at least a partial explanation of the paradox which Bene has described.

A Measure of Conflict

In order to explore more fully the conflicts found among grammar-school, as compared with modern-school children, the author carried out an inquiry in six schools in 1962. The concept of social role which has been developed by American sociologists and psychologists such as Merton[1] and Levinson[2] provides a valuable frame of reference for the interpretation of conflict situations. Social institutions confront their members with adaptive dilemmas, and these can be described in terms of the 'role-set'[3] and 'role-demand', 'role-conception' and 'role-performance'.[4] The predicaments of grammar-school and modern-school pupils were examined in these terms.

The role-demands and expectations made upon a person occupying a particular status (as wife, foreman, teacher, pupil, son, daughter etc.), may not coincide with the person's own conception of his role; and neither his conception nor the

---

[1] See R. K. Merton, 'Role-set: Problems in Sociological Theory', *British Journal of Sociology* (1957), **8**.
[2] See D. J. Levinson, 'Role, Personality, and Social Structure in the Organizational Setting', *Journal of Abnormal and Social Psychology* (1959), **58**.
[3] 'by role-set I mean that complement of role-relationships in which persons are involved by virtue of occupying a particular social status' (Merton).
[4] 'Role may be defined as the structurally given demands . . . associated with a given social position.' 'Role may be defined as the member's orientation or conception of the part that he is to play in the organization.' 'Role is commonly defined as the actions of the individual members—actions seen in terms of their relevance to the social structure . . .' (Levinson).

expectations of others may match his actual role performance. The size of the discrepancy between role-demands, role-conception, and role-performance is a measure of the conflict experienced by a person in a particular status. But this theoretical model is more complicated than a simple triangle of forces, for the role-demands are not necessarily in agreement: the role-set usually implies an array of possibly conflicting expectations. The individual may perceive not only that he cannot perform as he would wish, but that many people in significant social relationships with him expect him to perform differently.

No work is known to the author which attempts to quantify and measure the conflict or tension between role-demands, role-conception, and role-performance for individuals occupying particular statuses. He reports below his attempt to measure the conflicts of persons occupying the status of adolescent pupil.[1] The conception which schoolchildren and technical college students have of their role was compared with the demands which they perceived various adult authorities and their friends to make upon them, on the one hand, and with their perceptions of their own role performance, on the other.

There is no dearth of impressionistic accounts of conflict between adolescents and their parents and their peers. Margaret Mead[2] and David Riesman[3] have no doubt of their general and early capitulation to the expectations of their friends. Some doubt has been thrown on this picture by Morris[4] in England, and more recently by Riley, Riley and Moore[5] in their attempts to provide empirical verification for Riesman's hypotheses in America. Morris's inquiries into what adolescents thought they would or should do when there were conflicting demands from parents and peers led him seriously to question the potency of peer-group attraction and authority, and the tendency to adolescent conformity, in England; but he found rather more

---

[1] See F. Musgrove, 'Role-conflict in Adolescence', *British Journal of Educational Psychology* (1964), **34**.

[2] See Margaret Mead, 'Social Change and Cultural Surrogates' in C. Kluckhohn and H. A. Murray (eds.), *Personality in Nature, Society and Culture* (1948).

[3] D. Riesman, *The Lonely Crowd* (1950).

[4] J. F. Morris, 'The Development of Adolescent Value-Judgments', *British Journal of Educational Psychology* (1958), **28**.

[5] M. W. Riley, J. W. Riley and M. E. Moore, 'Adolescent Values and the Riesman Typology: An Empirical Analysis' in S. M. Lipset and L. Lowenthal (eds.), *Culture and Social Character* (1961).

inclination to conform to friends among secondary-modern than among grammar-school pupils.

Riley, Riley and Moore attempted to establish to what extent 2,500 middle-class American high-school students were 'other-' or 'inner-directed' by asking for their evaluation of 20 personality models or 'vignettes'. The vignettes represented 'Achievement Models', 'Good Time Models', and 'Peer Relations Models'. The subjects were asked to indicate those they themselves would like to resemble ('self-expectation'), those that they thought their popular coevals preferred as friends ('perceived peer expectations'), those they thought their parents wanted them to be like ('perceived parent expectations'), and those they thought it would be helpful to be like later on, after school ('adult self-expectation').

There was a tendency for these middle-class American adolescents to stand midway between the perceived expectations of friends and of parents: (for 67 per cent to prefer the 'success model', for example, while only 48 per cent of them thought that their friends wished them to resemble this model, but 80 per cent thought that their parents wished them to do so). There was a sense in which 'the adolescent's own values seem to form a bridge between the perceived other-direction of his peers and the perceived inner-and-other direction of his parents'.

The author's inquiry was carried out in the grammar school and a secondary modern school in each of three widely separated industrial towns in the North and the Midlands. Each town is engaged in mining and/or heavy industry with a population of approximately 40,000 inhabitants. Each town has a medium-sized grammar school recruited through orthodox selection procedures at 11-plus years. The secondary modern schools which co-operated in the research were also mixed. In addition one junior school and one college of technology were included in the inquiry.

A questionnaire was designed to make possible the measurement of role-conflict among the pupils in these eight educational institutions. The definition of adolescent role was derived from the author's inquiry into the self-pictures of adolescents, which is reported above in Chapter Five. Young people had been asked to complete in any way they wished which gave a true impression of their views, a sentence beginning 'Boys (or girls) of my age should . . .' Four areas of behaviour which were mentioned with great frequency were made the basis of the questionnaire:

1. 'Fit and good at games'.
2. 'Behave sensibly and generally "act your age" '.
3. 'Be respectful, courteous and polite to your parents and elders'.
4. 'Be quite free to stay up late, or to stay out late, if you wish'.

The four statements were taken to be descriptive of a generalized adolescent role-conception.

The subjects in this inquiry were asked to rank these four areas of behaviour to show what they ideally wished to be like ('role conception'), what they thought mothers, fathers, teachers, friends (and bosses in the case of part-time technical college students) respectively wished them to be like ('role-expectations'), and what they thought they were in fact like ('perceived role-performance'). Thus each subject was asked to place in the first column (Ideal Self) '1 against that statement which you would most like to apply to you, 4 against the statement which you are least bothered to be, 2 against the statement you would like to apply to you after number 1, and 3 against the statement you would like to apply to you after that'. Similar detailed instructions were given for the columns for 'Mother', 'Father', 'Teachers', 'Boss' and 'Friends': thus, 'In column 2 show what you think your father wants you to be like. Put 1 against the statement which you think he would most like you to be, 4 against what you think he is least bothered about, 2 against what you think he wants you to be after number 1, and 3 after that.' For the column relating to 'Actual Self' the instructions were: 'In column 6 put 1 against the statement which you think as a matter of fact fits you best, put 4 against the statement which you think as a matter of fact fits you least, 2 and 3 against the statements which fit you second and third.'

By computing Kendall's coefficient of concordance[1] for the

---

[1] See M. G. Kendall, *Rank Correlation Methods* (1948), pp. 80–9.

$$\text{The coefficient of concordance (W)} = \frac{12S}{m^2(n^3-n)}$$

where S = the sum of the squared differences between observed and expected ranks

m = the number of 'judges'

n = the number of ranks

six (or seven) ranks, a measure could be obtained for the degree of an individual's role conflict (ranging from 1·0, complete agreement between the ranks, to 0·0, total disagreement). By computing the coefficient for the perceived expectations of all three (or four) adults, a measure could be obtained for the felt congruence of demands from different adult authorities. Differences in measured conflict could be established between age-groups, sex-groups, and between adolescents of the same sex and age in different types of educational institution. The occupations of subjects' fathers were also obtained, and these were graded on the Registrar-General's scale of occupations (Class III being subdivided into IIIA, routine non-manual, and IIIB, skilled manual). It was thus possible to establish the extent of role-conflict in different social-class groups in different types of school.

Conflict in Grammar and Modern School Pupils

The questionnaire was completed by the children in the fourth year of the grammar schools (N = 275) and in the fourth year of the modern schools (N = 194); by the 47 children in the last year of the junior school; and by 69 male students aged 17 to 20, following part-time courses for professional qualifications in engineering in the technical college. The average age of the secondary-school boys and girls was 15 years, of the junior-school children, 11 years.

The greatest degree of conflict was found among grammar-school boys and the technical college students, the least among secondary-modern girls and junior-school children. Grammar-school girls and secondary-modern school boys occupied an intermediate position.

Comparisons were made by calculating the coefficient of concordance, W, for each pupil in a random sample of one in two from each sex-group in every institution. Although there were highly significant differences between types of school, there were no differences between the grammar-school children in the three towns, or between the secondary-modern children. The results for grammar schools are therefore combined, and for modern schools.

Role-conflict in Adolescence

TABLE XII

PERCENTAGE OF PUPILS AT THREE LEVELS OF CONFLICT

Value of W	Gr. Boys (N 64)	Mod. Boys (N 50)	Gr. Girls (N 78)	Mod. Girls (N 49)	Tech. Boys (N 35)	Jun. Boys (N 12)	Jun. Girls (N 12)
High conflict (0·00—0·33)	56·3	32·0	39·7	12·2	57·1	16·7	8·3
Medium conflict (0·34—0·66)	39·1	44·0	35·9	20·4	34·3	16·7	41·7
Low conflict (0·67—1·00)	4·6	24·0	24·0	67·4	8·6	66·6	50·0

More grammar-school than modern-school boys showed high levels of role-conflict,[1] more grammar-school girls than secondary-modern school girls.[2] The technical college students showed the same high levels of conflict as the grammar-school boys, and the latter greater conflict than the grammar-school girls.[3] The grammar-school girls did not differ significantly from the modern-school boys, but the latter showed greater conflict than modern-school girls.[4] Junior boys showed less conflict than modern-school boys,[5] but neither junior-school boys nor junior-school girls differed significantly from the low level of conflict found in the modern-school girls. When W was calculated from the median ranks for both sex groups in each type of school, the following coefficients were obtained: grammar-school boys 0·25,[6] technical college students 0·32,[7] grammar-school girls 0·37[8] secondary-modern boys 0·33,[9] secondary-modern girls 0·63,[10] junior-school boys 0·66,[11] and junior-school girls 0·96.[12]

No evidence was found in this inquiry to support the view

[1] $\chi^2 = 26·0$, d.f. $= 2$, $P<0·001$.
[2] $\chi^2 = 23.33$, d.f. $= 2$, $P<0·001$.
[3] $\chi^2 = 10·80$, d.f. $= 2$, $P<0·01$.
[4] $\chi^2 = 18·7$, d.f. $= 2$, $P<0·001$.
[5] $\chi^2 = 8·95$, d.f. $= 2$, $P<0·05$.
[6] Not significant.
[7] Not significant.
[8] Not significant.
[9] Not significant.
[10] Significant at the 0·01 level: F $= 8·5$, d.f. $= 2$. $66/13·30$; $F_{0·01} = 6·0$.
[11] Significant at the 0·01 level: F $= 9·3$, d.f. $= 2$. $66/13·30$; $F_{0·01} = 6·0$.
[12] Significant at the 0·01 level: F $= 9·5$, d.f. $= 2$. $66/13·30$; $F_{0·01} = 6·0$.

that working-class children in grammar schools experience greater conflict than middle-class children. Thus in one grammar school the coefficient of concordance calculated from the median rankings made by 22 middle-class boys (whose fathers were placed in the Registrar-General's occupational grades I–IIIA) was 0·12; but for all the boys in the school the value was 0·10. The coefficient for 28 middle-class girls in another grammar school was 0·17, for all the girls in the school 0·22. The value of W for 12 boys from white-collar homes in one modern school was 0·88, for all the boys in the school 0·69; the value of W for 10 'white-collar' girls in a modern school was 0·60, for all girls in the school 0·81.

No group perceived marked differences in the demands of the various adult figures, fathers, mothers, teachers, and, where applicable, bosses. 'Behave sensibly and generally "act your age"' and 'Be respectful, courteous and polite to your parents and elders' were seen as the prime expectations of all adults: the median rank accorded by all groups of subjects was either one or two. All groups saw all adults as placing 'Fit and good at games' third in importance, and being 'Quite free to stay up late, or to stay out late, if you wish' fourth.

On the other hand there was a high degree of conflict between the subjects' perceived expectations of their friends, their own preferred behaviour, and their conception of their actual behaviour. This conflict was much greater among grammar-school (and technical college) students than among modern-school pupils and centred particularly on being 'courteous etc., to parents and elders' and being 'free to stay up, or to stay out, late'.

The grammar-school boys saw 'being free to stay up, or to stay out, late' as an important expectation of their friends (median rank 2); ideally they attached little importance to this in their own behaviour (median rank 4); but they perceived their own behaviour midway between their ideal and the expectation of their friends (median rank 3). There was a similar conflict over being polite and respectful to parents and elders: ideally they rated this high, saw their friends as rating it low, and gave it an intermediate ranking as a feature of their actual behaviour. Secondary-modern girls (and to a smaller extent secondary-modern boys) showed less conflict over both areas of behaviour: they did not attach much importance to staying out late, they did not rate this as an outstanding feature of their actual behaviour, and did not see it as a prime demand by their friends. They saw their friends attaching the same high importance to respect and politeness to parents and elders that they did themselves.

TABLE XIII

CONFLICT BETWEEN IDEAL SELF, ACTUAL SELF, AND FRIENDS

'*Be respectful, courteous, polite*' etc.
(Median Ranks)

Subjects	Ideal Self	Actual Self	Friends
Grammar Boys (N 123)	2	3	4
Grammar Girls (N 152)	2	2	3
Modern Boys (N 99)	2	2	3
Modern Girls (N 95)	2	2	2

'*Be quite free to stay out late*' etc.

Grammar Boys	4	3	2
Grammar Girls	3	3	2
Modern Boys	4	4	3
Modern Girls	4	4	3

The median rankings of adults' expectations over the four areas of behaviour were in close agreement; the median rankings for ideal self, actual self, and friends, showed a high degree of conflict:

TABLE XIV

AGREEMENT BETWEEN ADULT EXPECTATIONS, CONFLICT BETWEEN SELF AND FRIENDS

	Grammar (B)	Technical (B)	Grammar (G)	Modern (B)	Modern (G)
W_a	0·80	0·90	0·93	0·85	0·85
$W_{si, sa, f}$	0·18	0·07	0·18	0·09	0·53

Legend: a = adults; si = self, ideal; sa = self, actual; f = friends

Sex groups in different types of school differed in the conflict in their perceived demands of adults, friends, and their ideal selves; but even when the expectations did not conflict, they differed in the weight which they saw friends, parents, teachers and themselves attaching to the four items of behaviour. Grammar-school boys themselves attached more weight to being fit and good at games than did modern-school boys; and more than the latter they saw their friends as making demands in this direction. Grammar-school boys saw adults as having a greater expectation that they should 'act their age', and friends a smaller expectation that they should be courteous and polite to their parents and elders. Modern-school boys attached more

TABLE XV

SIGNIFICANT DIFFERENCES BETWEEN GRAMMAR AND MODERN PUPILS
IN PERCEIVED EXPECTATIONS

(Percentages ranking an area of behaviour high: 1 or 2)

| Area of Behaviour | Boys | | | |
	Grammar (N 123)	Modern (N 99)	χ^2	P
'Fit and good at games'				
Ideal Self	60·8	47·5	6·10	0·05
Friends	80·5	55·5	16·20	0·001
'Sensible and "act your age"'				
Adults	88·1	74·1	18·85	0·001
Friends	28·4	51·5	11·50	0·001
'Respectful, polite etc.'				
Ideal Self	56·1	76·7	10·35	0·01
Friends	12·2	37·3	18·93	0·001
'Stay up or stay out late'				
Friends	94·3	57·3	11·34	0·001

| Area of Behaviour | Girls | | | |
	Grammar (N 152)	Modern (N 95)	χ^2	P
'Fit and good at games'				
Ideal Self	27·0	9·5	8·34	0·01
Friends	40·1	25·2	5·57	0·05
'Sensible and "act your age"'				
Friends	57·9	77·0	9·25	0·01
'Respectful, polite etc.'				
Friends	31·5	67·3	29·50	0·001
'Stay up or stay out late'				
Ideal Self	38·8	9·5	16·86	0·001
Friends	65·8	29·5	30·80	0·001

importance to respect and politeness in their own ideal behaviour, and saw their friends attaching less importance to their freedom to stay up or to stay out late.

Like the grammar-school boys, grammar-school girls attached greater weight than the modern-school girls to being good at games, and saw their friends as having a higher expectation in this regard. They saw their friends as attaching less importance to 'acting your age' and to being polite and showing respect. They attached more importance to being able to stay out late, and saw their friends as placing more weight on their being able to do so.

Like the middle-class adolescents in the American inquiry reported by Riley, Riley and Moore, both grammar-school boys and girls constituted, in their ideal conception of themselves, a bridge between the widely different demands they perceived from adults on the one hand, and from friends on the other. This was not so generally the case with secondary-modern school boys, and still less with secondary-modern girls.

TABLE XVI

SELF-CONCEPTION IN RELATION TO PERCEIVED
EXPECTATIONS OF ADULTS AND OF FRIENDS
(Percentage Ranking an Area High: 1 or 2)

	I—Games			II—Sensible			III—Polite			IV—Out late		
	A	S	F	A	S	F	A	S	F	A	S	F
GR (B) N 123	19	60	80	88	54	28	90	56	12	3	30	94
MOD (B) N 99	28	47	55	74	50	51	85	77	37	8	26	57
GR (G) N 152	14	27	40	94	67	58	96	74	31	2	39	66
MOD (G) N 95	15	9	25	87	90	77	91	87	67	4	9	29

Legend: A = Perceived expectations of adults
S = Self-expectation
F = Perceived expectations of friends
GR = Grammar School
MOD = Modern school

This table shows not only where 'self-expectation' is located in relation to the perceived expectations of adults and of friends, but the 'spread' of conflict—particularly wide with grammar-school boys, particularly narrow with modern-school girls. The latter were much nearer to the expectations of adults than of friends; in general the former are nearer in their preferred behaviour to the perceived expectations of friends than of adults. Morris found, in the research to which reference has already been made, that there was rather more 'conformity to friends' among secondary-modern than among grammar-school pupils. It is true that the present inquiry shows that grammar-school boys (and to a lesser extent grammar-school girls) are 'further from' their friends than their counterparts in the modern schools. But they are also much further from adults.

In particular the grammar-school boy's role-conception is remote from the perceived role-expectations of adults and friends: he is at the point of maximum tension. At the other extreme the secondary-modern school girl's role-conception is close to the perceived role-expectations of both adults and friends. Thus while 19·2 per cent of grammar-school boys thought that adults had a high expectation of their being fit and good at games, while as many as 80·5 per cent thought their friends had this high expectation, an intermediate proportion, 60·2 per cent, rated this as important in their ideal behaviour. But modern-school girls were not a 'bridge', in this sense, between adults and friends. While 9·5 per cent attached importance to being fit and good at games, 15·4 per cent thought that adults had a high expectation of this, and 25·2 per cent thought that their friends had. Whereas the spread of conflict for the modern-school girls (the difference between highest and lowest perceived expectations) was only 15·7 per cent, for the grammar-school boys the spread of conflict over this area of behaviour was 61·3 per cent.

The Roots of Conflict

The interpretation of these findings can be only speculative. The role-conflicts of boys were consistently very high in three widely separated grammar schools; the role-conflicts of girls in three modern schools in the same areas were consistently very low. Intermediate in degree were the role-conflicts of grammar-school girls and secondary-modern boys. Grammar-school boys and girls were significantly more at odds with themselves, with their friends and with teachers, mothers and fathers, than were their counterparts in the modern schools. These results are consistent with the surprising findings of Bene, which are discussed above.

The research of Hallworth[1] into the anxieties of modern- and grammar-school children might lead us to expect that grammar schools select personalities *already* prone to self-blame, self-criticism, and hypercritical attitudes to others. (He found that grammar-school children were not more generally anxious, but more given to self-blame, more socially introverted and prone to 'thinking introversion'.) This might suggest, in Freudian terms, that 'good grammar-school material' is characterized by a highly developed superego which has its foundations in infancy and early childhood. But if this were the explanation of these findings which have been reported above, we might reasonably expect that those children in the junior school who had been assessed to have the intelligence, level of attainment and academic aptitude for a grammar-school education would already experience more role-conflict than their 'unselected' contemporaries. This was not the case. Two boys and five girls in the junior school had been selected for grammar-school places: they were from various social levels, their fathers being an electrician, a van driver, a greengrocer, a skilled factory operative, a baker, a hosiery knitter, and a fitter respectively. The coefficients of concordance for these children were as high as for their classmates: 0·83, 0·83, 0·61, 0·83, 0·87, 0·88 and 0·95.

It seems probable that it is the experience of a particular type of educational institution, perhaps in conjunction with pre-existing personality traits, which promotes or reduces role-conflict. The grammar school and the technical college, which make extreme demands upon their pupils and emphasize their dependence and protracted exclusion from full involvement in adult affairs, may induce a deeper sense of conflict than the modern school, with its more moderate demands and more intimate relationship, particularly for the 14- and 15-year-olds, with the adult world. The male technical-college students were older than the grammar- and modern-school pupils, and had

---

[1] H. J. Hallworth, 'Anxiety in Secondary Modern and Grammar School Pupils', *British Journal of Educational Psychology* (1961), 31.

come from both modern and grammar schools; yet irrespective of their previous education their role-conflicts were as extreme as those found among the grammar-school boys.

It is true that local and national surveys of the leisure-pursuits of the young have found no marked differences between the extent to which modern- and grammar-school pupils make contact with adult life through part-time paid employment. The Crowther Report (1960) found that 53 per cent of grammar-school boys had part-time employment before leaving school, 55 per cent of the modern-school boys; 30 per cent of grammar-school girls (mainly as shop assistants on Saturdays), but only 17 per cent of modern-school girls.[1] Nevertheless, there are indications that senior modern-school pupils are more heavily involved in, and psychologically committed to, part-time activities in co-operation with adults than are grammar-school pupils, who tend more often to spend their leisure in the segregated world of juvenile sport, youth clubs, and other forms of formal youth organization.

Inquiries among the young people of Ilford have shown that gardening was the favourite out-of-school activity of only 5 per cent of grammar-school boys, but of 16 per cent of modern-school boys.[2] There are studies carried out in Birmingham,[3] Lancashire,[4] and Cardiff[5] which show the very considerable extent to which modern-school girls help in domestic duties, particularly at the weekend. Grammar-school pupils tend, on the other hand, to associate with their coevals in clubs. The Crowther Committee found, for example, that only 21 per cent of the ex-grammar-school boys in their survey belonged to no youth club, but 44 per cent of ex-modern-school boys were members of no club.[6] It is probably a mistake to regard the jobs which modern-

[1] *15 to 18*: Central Advisory Council for Education (England) (1960), pp. 30–1. Cf. J. D. Watson, *The Use of Leisure* (1962), unpub. thesis for Diploma in the Social Psychology of Education, University of Leicester. 51 per cent of a sample of 14–15 year old modern school boys in Rugby had regular part-time employment. School, rather than work, was the part-time activity.

[2] See M. Stewart, 'Leisure Activities of Grammar School Children', *British Journal of Educational Psychology* (1950), 20.

[3] W. Curr, et al., 'How Secondary Modern School Children Spend Their Time', *Educational Review* (1962), 15.

[4] L. M. Smalley, 'A Practicable Diary Technique for Time Sampling the Everyday Life of Children', *Educational Review* (1958), 10.

[5] A. Crichton, et al., 'Youth and Leisure in Cardiff', *Sociological Review* (1962), 10.

[6] Op. cit., Table 29a, p. 86.

school boys and girls do alongside adults as irksome chores: they give a sense of usefulness and importance to the concerns of the grown-up world. Youth-club membership underlines non-adult status, dependence and exclusion from the 'real' world. Modern-school boys and girls allow themselves to suffer comparatively little from this indignity.

But the grammar-school pupil's comparatively unhappy outlook on life, society and himself is probably caused more by his experiences at school than outside. He is under greater pressure to work hard and achieve high; and his teachers' attitudes are probably more distant and aloof. In contrast is Mays's account of the relaxed, open and cheerful attitudes of modern-school pupils even in the 'tough' and forbidding schools of down-town Liverpool: 'The schoolchildren today look more cheerful, are more forthcoming, less withdrawn, less cowed, more friendly and self-confident than at any time in the past, of which we have reliable knowledge . . . The schools are happier places even if the children are less attuned to hard work . . .'[1]

The author's own inquiries into teachers' conceptions of their role indicate that teachers in modern schools place far more emphasis on social training, and are more concerned about the nature and quality of their social relationships with their pupils, than are grammar-school teachers, who conceive their task in narrowly intellectual terms. (Similar disregard for personal relationships appears to characterize university teachers, at least in the provincial universities. 'There is a terrific gap between staff and students which shouldn't be. It's just like school' runs a typical student comment at Manchester.[2]) When the teachers of 4 grammar schools and 14 modern schools ranked 6 educational objectives in order of importance,[3] the modern-school teachers gave priority to moral and social training, grammar-school teachers to instruction in school subjects. The grammar-school

[1] J. B. Mays, *Education and the Urban Child* (1962), pp. 86–7. Cf. '. . . there are no indications whatsoever that the children attending the down-town schools are under severe pressure. Indeed, there are reasons for believing that they view their school careers too lightly . . .' (p. 198).

[2] See 'No One Speaks to You: Cold Shoulders at Manchester', *Times Educational Supplement*, 23 November 1962, p. 682: report of an inquiry into staff-student relationships at Manchester University.

[3] 1. Moral training; 2. Instruction in a subject or subjects; 3. Social training; 4. Education for family life and parenthood; 5. Social advancement; 6. Education for citizenship.

teachers also conceived their role more narrowly: they were significantly more often inclined to indicate items in the list of educational objectives as none of their business. (They also experienced less role-conflict than modern-school teachers: perhaps for this reason their pupils experience more.) It is perhaps to the greater social distance between teachers and pupils in orthodox grammar schools that we must look for an explanation of the extreme role-conflicts of grammar-school boys and girls.

Chapter Seven

YOUTH AND SOCIAL CHANGE

Frustration and Innovation

WHEN, in the days of World War II, Karl Mannheim looked forward to a reconstructed post-war Britain, he emphasized the important role that youth must play if progress and change were to be achieved. 'I believe that static societies which develop only gradually, and in which the rate of change is relatively slow, will rely mainly on the experience of the old.'[1] A dynamic society, on the other hand, would accord youth a high status: a frustrated and stagnant Britain had failed to give youth 'its proper place and share in public life.'[2] Although Mannheim was aware that the driving force of the young originated in large measure from their 'outsider' position,[3] he saw no inconsistency in urging that they should become insiders: 'the dynamic societies which want to make a new start, whatever their social or political philosophy may be, will rely mainly on the co-operation of youth. They will organize their vital resources and will use them in breaking down the established direction of social development.'

The truth is probably the opposite of Mannheim's thesis. It is true that high status of young people is often closely associated with a heightened tempo of social change; but it is frequently a consequence rather than a cause. Eisenstadt has pointed to great social and political movements in nineteenth-century Europe which were closely associated with the energies of young people —Mazzini's 'Young Italy', the German youth movements following the rapid transformation which took place during the post-Bismarckian era; and the nationalist movements in the Near and Far East today which have relied heavily on students and young

[1] Karl Mannheim, *Diagnosis of Our Time* (1943), p. 33.
[2] Ibid., p. 43.
[3] Ibid., p. 36.

army officers.[1] But the latter have achieved importance after the social and political revolutions and not before: it was their low status in the traditional, familistic setting, in which the authority of the elders was paramount, which must be seen as an important cause of social change; their subsequent high status is a result. It is likely that revolutionary change which owes much to such circumstances will fail to maintain its forward momentum.[2] The middle- and upper-class young women of late-Victorian and Edwardian England, whose status frustrations led to the militant Suffragette movement, have been succeeded in mid-twentieth-century Britain by an enfranchised adult female population unremarkable at any social level for vigorous, let alone revolutionary, political activity.

The causes of social change are complex, and the low status of youth only one factor which merits attention. But it is a factor which has been comparatively little examined. When the modes of social change which have occurred among non-literate peoples in contact with the West are compared, the position of the young in the indigenous societies provides at least a partial explanation of the nature of the response. It is now many years since Fortes argued that a comparative sociology of culture contact was needed 'without which we can never hope to perceive the causes of social change.'[3] In this chapter nothing so ambitious is attempted; but a variety of circumstances in which social change has occurred—or has been resisted—will be compared, and as far as possible the status of the young isolated and examined for its bearing on the processes of resistance and change.

The argument advanced in this chapter is this: that in those societies in which the status of adolescents and young adults (particularly the males) is high, change will tend to be slow, the blandishments of an elaborate and alien civilization resisted; where their status is low, and their seniors can effectively block their access to adult statuses and impede their assumption of

---

[1] S. N. Eisenstadt, *From Generation to Generation* (1956), pp. 171–4.
[2] Cf. A. J. P. Taylor's interpretation of the failure of German liberals in 1848—because they had succeeded, as students, in the movement of national liberation in 1813: 'The revolution of 1848 was not the explosion of new forces, but the belated triumph of *Burschenschaft*, the students of the war of liberation who were now men in their fifties . . . dependent on the princes for their salaries or pensions as civil servants.' See *The Course of German History* (1945), p. 69.
[3] Meyer Fortes, 'Culture Contact as a Dynamic Process', *Africa* (1936), 9.

adult roles, then there is likely to be a predisposition to change, to social innovation and experimentation, to a ready response to the opportunities which may be offered by an alien, intrusive culture to follow alternative and quicker routes to power and importance. When the young are segregated from the adult world, held in low esteem, and delayed in their entry into adult life, they are likely to constitute a potentially deviant population; but when they are segregated from the adult world in a position of high status and power (for instance, in warrior groups), a conservative society is the probable result. High status and a sense of importance may be achieved by the young through integration with, rather than segregation from, the adult world: they may share their seniors' work and responsibilities, their pleasures and pastimes; in this case, too, resistance to change is likely to be strong.

While British anthropologists of the 'functional' school have resolutely refused to invoke psychology to account for the processes of culture change, finding sufficient explanation in 'social facts', in the inter-relations of institutions and their capacity or incapacity to satisfy 'needs', American anthropologists have looked for light in personality- and in learning-theory. 'A well-developed learning theory,' Hallowell has maintained, 'is relevant to promoting further knowledge of the whole process of cultural transmission as well as the processes involved in acculturation and culture change.'[1] The new learning which takes place when social change occurs, it is argued, is explicable only in terms of the personality organization which facilitates or impedes adjustment to new circumstances: in the process of social change, 'a crucial variable may be the kind of personality structure of the people undergoing acculturation.'[2]

While it is true that sociological explanations imply at least rudimentary psychological assumptions—usually somewhat crudely hedonistic views of learning and motivation—it is possible to look for the social correlates of change without venturing into the wide sea of personality-and-culture theory. The position of the young in a society's social structure can be shown to have an intimate connection with that society's stability

[1] A. Irving Hallowell, 'Culture, Personality, and Society', in A. L. Kroeber, *Anthropology Today* (1953), p. 599.
[2] Ibid., pp. 613–14.

and response to changing external circumstances. It is true that throughout the world today non-literate societies are changing whatever may be the power enjoyed by their young; but their rates and modes of change differ, and their readiness or proneness to change have varied widely at the 'zero point of contact' (in Lucy Mair's phrase), even when the alien impact was similar in range, intensity, organization, and content. The standardized policy of America's Indian Affairs Department in the later nineteenth century met with a wide variety of reactions from the Indian tribes: the Makah[1] were remarkable for their degree of assimilation to American culture while remaining active and vigorous; the Sioux,[2] treated to an essentially similar programme of education and Americanization, rejected the alien culture, without vigour, only with dispirited apathy. The tribes of Africa have shown a similar variety of response to the endeavours of European missionaries, labour recruiters, and government officials.

Change may be voluntary or forced,[3] but however reluctant in their first encounter, tribal societies throughout the world are undergoing change, at varying rates. The size and concentration of their populations, their proximity to or remoteness from European institutions and settlements, the administrative policies of imperial powers, are all relevant circumstances. Tribes in which the cultivation of cash crops has been successfully introduced have probably made the most important and positive changes in adapting tribal life to a new political and economic context;[4] tribes which supply migrant labour to distant European enterprises have often changed less; those with neither cash cropping nor migrant labourers have generally persisted in a traditional way of life. But at the zero point of impact, tribal societies showed marked differences in their proneness to change, even when the impact was similar in nature and extent.

When Her Majesty's Special Commissioner made his preliminary report on the Uganda Protectorate in 1900, he was struck by the different responses of tribes within a relatively small

[1] See Elizabeth Colson, *The Makah Indians* (1953).
[2] See G. MacGregor, *Warriors without Weapons* (1946).
[3] For a useful discussion of this distinction, see Ian Hogbin, *Social Change* (1958), pp. 98-9.
[4] See A. Southall, 'Social Change, Demography and Extrinsic Factors' in A. Southall (ed.), *Social Change in Modern Africa* (1961), pp. 1-13.

region of Africa. 'Among the naked Nilotic negroes of the
eastern half of the Protectorate missionary propaganda seems at
the present time to be absolutely impossible . . . On the other
hand, the Bantu-speaking natives are well inclined to religious
inquiry.'[1] The egalitarian Lango and Iteso, without marked
distinctions of rank or political authority ('it is sometimes difficult
to find a man who does not profess to be a "somebody" '[2]),
were contemptuous of alien ideas, institutions, and customs,
tenacious of their own; the hierarchical, centralized states like
the Baganda, among whom distinctions of rank and age were
marked, and the track of seniority long, were more ready to learn
alien ways. From the very first days of contact they showed
themselves not only predisposed to learn a new religion,[3] but
were 'greedy for cloth and for almost every manufactured article
up to a phonograph and a brougham.'[4]

When a social system presents blockages and delays to the
satisfaction of needs, particularly the urgently felt social and
sexual needs of young men, the institutions of an alien civilization
may be eagerly embraced. The new institutions may, indeed,
create new needs,[5] but initially they offer the chance of satisfying
existing needs more quickly and directly. 'An individual adopts
an innovation of his own free will only when he has become
convinced that it offers him some kind of reward—perhaps
greater efficiency, or more security, or enhanced status.'[6] An
established value may now be realized more effectively in a new
way;[7] thus whereas security, land, status and the brideprice

[1] *Preliminary Report of Her Majesty's Special Commissioner on the Uganda Protectorate*
(1901), cd. 671, p. 6.
[2] A. L. Kitching, *On the Backwaters of the Nile* (1912), p. 160.
[3] Even at the price of martyrdom at the hands of political superiors who interpreted
the new learning as a threat to their authority. See R. P. Ashe, *Two Kings of Uganda*
(1899), pp. 215–31, for an account of kabaka Mwanga's persecution of native
Christians ('readers') in Buganda.
[4] *Preliminary Report . . . on the Uganda Protectorate* (1901).
[5] See the author's study, 'A Uganda School as a Field of Culture Change', *Africa*
(1952), **22**, for an examination of an African school as an institution which meets
'emergent needs' which have no strict counterpart in either the indigenous or the
intrusive culture.
[6] Ian Hogbin, op. cit., p. 57.
[7] Ibid., p. 94. Cf. B. Malinowski, *The Dynamics of Culture Change* (1945): 'One kind
of institution can be replaced by another which fulfils a similar function' (p. 52).
'The ultimate reality in culture change thus hinges on the fact that corresponding
institutions in two cultures satisfy analagous needs in different ways and with
different techniques . . .' (p. 71).

could eventually be attained by young men throughout most of Melanesia through service to maternal uncles, Western contact offered an alternative and quicker route to independence and fully adult status: work for wages in European enterprises. The result is to undermine the authority of age: 'the senior men are in a quandary . . . The tendency is therefore towards a loosening of the ties binding the two age-groups together.'[1]

New institutions may be accepted because they seem to lend support to existing social values; but their long term effect may be to undermine them. Thus European-type schools have often been supported by African parents because their immediate effect has been to discipline the young and maintain the authority of seniority. In the nineteen-thirties Lucy Mair found in the villages of Buganda that:

The parents themselves are anxious to have their children go to school; there is no question of the children being taken from their influence against their will . . . The parents do not themselves feel that European education is likely to make their children disrespectful. Indeed I remember one father declaring that children were better kept in order at school than at home . . .'[2]

But the boys themselves may welcome school not because it supports (some of) the traditional values of the indigenous social order, but because it subverts them. As the author reported from Uganda in the nineteen-fifties: 'The school appears to be most effective (with its pupils) when it is not attempting to take over the functions of tribal institutions: it is most effective not in shoring up the deficiencies of tribal institutions, but when it is on wholly new ground, dealing with subjects outside the sphere of traditional instruction and pursuits.'[3]

The Wilsons presented a cataclysmic view of social change under conditions of culture contact. Seeing pre-contact African societies as coherent systems ("To deny the assumption of social coherence would be to abandon all hope of analysis in

[1] Ian Hogbin, op. cit., p. 94.
[2] L. P. Mair, *An African People in the Twentieth Century* (1934), pp. 68–9.
[3] F. Musgrove, 'Some Reflections on the Sociology of African Education', *African Studies* (1952), 11. See also the author's study of African children's play: '(they) do not of their own accord bring traditional games into the school': 'Education and the Culture Concept', *Africa* (1953), 23.

history . . .'[1]), albeit with 'normal opposition' which could be contained—between a boy and his mother's brother, between co-wives or a wife and her husband's people—they argued that culture contact introduced 'radical opposition', fundamental and irreconcilable conflict between law and law, logic and logic, convention and convention. Social change was disequilibrium: thus Christianity and monogamy raised complex opposition within the society of the Nyakyusa: the traditional value of hospitality by the wealthy was incapable of realization with such institutions, 'The opposition can only be removed by social change, economic or religious.'[2]

But social change had already occurred—when some, at least, of the Nyakyusa adopted Christianity and monogamy: what the Wilson's are perhaps explaining is *further* social change. The initial acceptance of new institutions—which may have unforseen consequences in the future—when it is voluntary, is a solution to existing tensions and frustrations. When marriage is an important sign of adult status, and when the conditions of marriage are closely controlled by the older age groups, change may be accepted because it promotes an existing value (status through marriage) while undermining another (the authority of the old). At least for the young the balance of advantage is on the side of change: they have not even necessarily learned new ideas and values, but have only found support for ideas and values which already existed, but were perhaps experimental and disreputable. Discontent with the authority of their seniors was already present. 'Every real society consists of a core of orthodox norms and conforming actions round the margins of which continuous experiment goes on. It is from the margins of experiment that changing norms and actions emerge into sanctioned acceptance.'[3]

Societies which have shown an initial proneness to change have often been characterized by the frustrations of young men whose chance of marriage is jeopardized by the power of elderly polygynists. The Mende of Sierra Leone and the Azande of the Sudan have been differently involved in contact with the West: the former have had a more sustained and intimate contact, the

[1] G. and M. Wilson, *Analysis of Social Change* (1945), p. 23.
[2] Ibid., p. 126.
[3] A. W. Southall, 'Norms and Status Symbols' in A. W. Southall (ed.) *Social Change in Modern Africa* (1961), p. 14.

latter are geographically remote. Both are societies hierarchical in their social and political organization, both give power to older men, and both have been noted for their inclination to social innovation and their ready acceptance of change. Formerly among the Azande 'The older men had a monopoly of wives, and in the past it was difficult for young men to marry. The need of food and the hope of acquiring a sufficient number of spears with which to marry anchored a youth to his family and kin. The father of a family exercised great control over his sons who treated him with deep respect.'[1] Similarly with the Mende: 'Married persons constitute a definite and more senior category to those who are unmarried irrespective of the actual age of the latter.' 'In the old days, few men had the opportunity of obtaining a wife before they were 30, or even 35 years of age, and had proved their hardihood and diligence. Nowadays . . . a man has more opportunities to secure the amount of bridewealth through his own efforts and so achieve a wife while still in his early twenties.'[2] In such circumstances the young have every reason to enter the mission school, European factory and mine.

Segregation with High Status

The societies which have shown themselves particularly resistant to change at least in the early phases of their contact with the culture of the West have commonly been those in which the young had a high and assured status and importance either through their close involvement in adult affairs or through segregated age-group institutions which exercised social, political or military power. Segregated age-group organizations of this kind are to be found in tribes widely different in their political and social structures; and the precise functions of the age-groups are themselves extremely various. They are found in 'segmentary tribes' without central governmental institutions—the Nuer, the Nandi, the Plains Indians, the Lango and the Masai; they are

---

[1] E. E. Evans-Pritchard, *Witchcraft and Oracles among the Azande* (1937), p. 16. 'We shall find that social status intrudes into every phase of Azande life' (p. 14), but 'it is unusually easy for the European to establish contact with them . . . (they) are always ready to copy the behaviour of those they regard as their superiors in culture and to borrow new modes of dress, new weapons and utensils, new words, and even new ideas . . .' (p. 13).

[2] K. L. Little, *The Mende of Sierra Leone* (1951), p. 140.

found in centralized kingdoms like the Zulu and the Ashanti. The structure and the functions of the age-groups[1] vary: the age-range embraced, their internal sub-divisions and organization, their political, educational, military or social activities and purposes. Thus the Nandi age-set[2] of young men has military significance, but the age-set system of the Nuer of the Sudan has neither a military nor a political purpose: it is a major determinant of social relationships and domestic behaviour.[3] But in all cases initiation is associated with the legitimate entry into heterosexual relationships; membership of the age-group promotes status in the total community (as opposed to the family or other local group) and so functions as an integrative mechanism for the entire society. Although the anthropological evidence on change in these different tribes is often difficult to compare, and the ways of *measuring* social change so various as to make comparison particularly difficult, these societies do appear to have shown unusual persistence in their traditional ways even under considerable external pressure. Speaking of such societies Eisenstadt has observed: 'The existing data fully warrant the assumption that no *structural* tendencies towards deviancy can be discerned in these age groups . . .'[4]

The Nandi and the Nuer are both tribes whose conservatism has been fully attested and whose age-group organizations have been thoroughly and meticulously investigated and described. Nuer youths are initiated at the age of 14 to 16; they then jump 'from the grade of boyhood to the grade of manhood, and the character of their social life is correspondingly transformed . . .' 'After initiation a lad takes on the full privileges and obligations of manhood in work, play, and war. Above all, he gives himself whole-heartedly to winning the favours of the maidens of the neighbourhood.'[5] Adult status is not dependent on marriage. Sons are married by seniority, and after one has married the family herd must reach its former strength before cattle are

[1] 'Age-set' refers to persons who have been initiated during the successive annual ceremonies of a single initiation period; 'age-group' refers more generally to any division of a population by age. Political duties may be allocated on the basis of age: the age-sets then pass through the successive age-grades of warrior and elder.
[2] See G. W. B. Huntingford, *The Nandi of Kenya* (1953).
[3] See E. E. Evans-Pritchard, *The Nuer* (1940).
[4] S. N. Eisenstadt, op. cit., p. 280.
[5] E. E. Evans-Pritchard, *Kinship and Marriage among the Nuer* (1951), p. 51.

available for the marriage of the next. Thus a young man may not marry until his mid-twenties. In the meantime, however, he will have no problem of access to women.

Age-group membership, and particularly initiation, has been held to account more than anything else for the character and social attitudes of the Nuer: their sensitivity, pride and arrogance, their stubbornness and independence, their impatience of authority.[1] They have in the past shown no sense of inferiority in the presence of the white man, no inclination to adopt his institutions and way of life.

Similarly with the Nandi of Kenya. Proud and conservative, with a long history of resistance to British administration, they have been unwilling to change the customs, beliefs and outlook of their ancestors. Without chiefs or any form of central authority, the warrior age-set exercises great power. The age-range within an age-set might be 7 or 8 years. 10 to 15 years might elapse between the completion of one set and the opening of another. The initiates attain full adult status after a few months' seclusion; they have no need to wait until the completion of the 4-year initiation period. As warriors they can marry and make love to unmarried girls, they are responsible for military operations and enjoy wide social privileges. The younger boys' age-sets dance attendance on them, but they in their turn are assured of succession when power is formally handed over.[2]

The close connection between the power of the young and social stability is seen among the Comanche Indians when they moved from the Plateau to the Plains. In their earlier, inhospitable plateau environment they were a potentially unstable society. Dominated by the old, the young of very little account, the transformation of their culture has been described as a 'striking lesson in social change'.[3]

As a brigand tribe of the Plains, the young warriors on whom prosperity depended enjoyed a dominant social position; institutions evolved which promoted their cohesion and solidarity—wife-sharing, the equal distribution of spoils, the limited tenure of positions of leadership. 'These men exercised no formal civil authority, but they possessed great power through prestige. In

[1] See E. E. Evans-Pritchard, *The Nuer* (1940).
[2] G. W. B. Huntingford, op. cit.
[3] Abram Kardiner, *The Psychological Frontiers of Society* (1945).

reality they managed the tribe.' 'Top rank in Comanche society was attained by the fine warrior . . . When he was past the fighting age, his status declined quickly.'[1]

Forcible change was eventually brought to the Comanche ('they were retired under government protection'[2]). But until this happened, they had a stability which has been attributed largely to the fact that 'the individuals are not blocked in development, and the individual can contribute to the common good and participate in it according to his talents. It is a true democracy.'[3]

Other societies have accorded less power to organized youth but, while they have retained the direction of affairs in the hands of the elders, they have nevertheless given to youth a sense of importance and social usefulness. Among the Nyakyusa of Tanganyika the unique institution of the age-village segregates young males from adult society from the age of 9 or 10. The original members of the age-village remain together throughout life. Although in their early youth they are economically dependent on their fathers, whose fields they hoe, they have a sense of solidarity and power; they value good fellowship and co-operation; and although they are commoners, at least as they reach mature years they constitute a social and political force of which hereditary chiefs must take serious account.

The tension between the uprising and the mature generation is minimal. Inter-generation accusations of witchcraft are very rare.[4] Eisenstadt surprisingly includes the Nyakyusa among the 'familistic societies' in which, 'since these age groups arise as a result of strong tension between the generations, a somewhat stronger deviant potential is indicated.'[5] If the Nyakyusa age-groups originated in strong inter-generation tension, they have proved a most effective social mechanism for reducing it.[6]

[1] Ibid., pp. 55–6.
[2] Ibid., p. 96.
[3] Ibid., p. 423.
[4] See Monica Wilson, *Good Company* (1951).
[5] S. N. Eisenstadt, op. cit., p. 249.
[6] Cf. the argument that societies in which, because of child-rearing arrangements, young males are particularly hostile to their fathers and dependent on their mothers often resolve the conflict *either* through initiation ceremonies *or* through a change of residence for the boys at puberty. The Nuer, for example, are held to be an illustration of the former practice, the Nyakyusa of the latter: 'change of residence serves the same functions that we have posited for initiation ceremonies, for example, by establishing male authority, breaking the bond with the mother, and ensuring

Youth and Social Change

The Ngoni of Nyasaland also segregate their young males; and
here the connection between the pride and sense of importance
of young men on the one hand, and the society's conservatism
on the other, is perhaps easier to see. It is true that the proud,
hierarchical Ngoni, with their keen sense of social distinction and
precedence, are changing: economic developments have been
beyond their control, and 'The economic foundations of political
power and social prestige have been to a large extent undermined
by the abolition of war and slavery and the exodus of men to the
south for work in mines and on farms.'[1] But change has for long
been resisted. The initial reaction was one of 'pronounced
antipathy to European contact'. The traditional values and
customs have been overwhelmed rather than willingly
surrendered. The ancient virtues of dignity, self-control and
correct deportment are still valued and achieved in a changing
social order.

Personal dignity and self-esteem are in large measure the
outcome of life in the boys' dormitory, which young males enter
at the age of 6. Although the age-range in the dormitories was
formerly very wide, spanning more than a dozen years, and
internal distinctions of status were sharp, life in them promoted a
sense of solidarity and high morale. The boys were not segregated
in futile dependency: they had a valued contribution to make to
the life and economy of the nation.

They were of sufficient importance to be allowed into the
discussions of high affairs conducted by the senior men at the
kraal gate; in caring for cattle they did a responsible job from
which they gained a strong notion of their own importance.
Although marriage among the Ngoni was formerly comparatively
late—usually little short of 30 for men—adolescent and young
adult males seem to have had no sense of frustration or resentment against their elders. 'The seeming absence of frustration
and overt rebellion in the years just after puberty was due to the

[1] Margaret Read, *Native Standards of Living and African Culture Change* (1938).

acceptance of the male role.' The absence of both initiation ceremonies and of
residential change for adolescent males among the Tallensi, for example, is explained
according to this theory by different methods of infant care, particularly the shorter
period of exclusive mother-son sleeping arrangements. See J. W. M. Whiting,
R. Kluckhohn and A. Anthony, 'The Function of Male Initiation Ceremonies at
Puberty', in E. E. Maccoby, T. M. Newcomb and E. L. Hartley (eds.), *Readings in
Social Psychology* (3rd ed. 1958).

136

social recognition by relatives and by the village community of the new stage reached by boys and girls, and to the increasing responsibility required of them for carrying out allotted tasks and for preparing for their future careers.'[1]

Integration with High Status

Adolescents and young men may achieve a sense of high importance not from segregation in age-sets or looser age-groups associations which confer high status, power, or privilege, but from close connection with the lives and affairs of adults. Eisenstadt suggests that this absence of age-group organization is a feature of those societies—often 'segmentary' tribes—in which the kin group is a virtually self-sufficient social unit, in which the young can learn all the role dispositions necessary for adult life. Seniority may play an important part in the regulation of behaviour, but the young have an integral role in the social order.

The Tallensi of northern Ghana, the Tikopia of Polynesia, and perhaps the Samoans, are examples of societies which are on the whole conservative and in which the young have importance through social integration. The young of Tikopia in the nineteen-twenties, although before puberty they generally went around in independent little bands, were early involved in the central concerns of the island's economy. 'The child soon comes to take part in the work of the community, and so useful is it that a household without one is at a distinct loss. At first it goes out with a relative to the cultivations and intersperses its play with fetching and carrying things. Gradually most of the economic minutiae are allotted to it by its elders, including others than parents, and its performances, small in themselves, act as the emollient which allows the household machinery to run smoothly.'[2] Although marriage was relatively late and the authority of elders respected, Firth found no evidence of revolt or deviation among the young, who found ample compensation in their way of life and accepted the social institutions in which they were increasingly involved—mourning obligations, affinal regulations, and duties to chiefs.

[1] Margaret Read, *Children of their Fathers* (1959), p. 170.
[2] R. Firth, *We, the Tikopia* (1957 ed.), p. 150.

A quarter of a century later Firth found the Tikopia remarkably little changed in spite of their widening contacts with the outer world. In 1929 they had shown little inclination to go abroad to work for wages; by 1952 migrant labour was more common. But the influence of the West was incorporated into the existing social structure without appreciably changing it. 'The reaction was one of incorporation—to keep the fabric of the culture intact while using in it as many foreign elements as possible. "We, the Tikopia", wished to remain the Tikopia.'[1] Between 1929 and 1952 they had even 'incorporated' the use of money, using the white man's currency for dealing with the white man, the traditional currency (bark-cloth) for transactions among themselves.

In spite of the continued efforts of Christian missionaries there was as much polygamy in 1952 as in 1929 (though the proportion of polygamous marriages was small at both dates). There was no change in the actual quantity of marriage: while there had been an increase of 33 per cent in spouses of all kinds, the population had grown by 35 per cent. Marriage was still relatively late, but the sex intrigues of young unmarrieds were still common form. The system of descent was little changed, and young men still choose their brides from a very limited geographical range: in 1952 as in 1929 one-sixth of all marriages took place between people of the same village. Although Firth senses the likelihood of imminent widespread social change, little had in fact occurred since the time of his original field-work in the twenties.

Another Polynesian people, the Samoans, accord their young a position in society similar to that in Tikopia; and while they have proved a flexible and adaptable society, like the Tikopians they incorporated Western influence without undergoing drastic social transformation. When Margaret Mead investigated their social life in the twenties, she found that the young were given tasks, according to their strength and abilities, which were functionally related to the work of the adult world. Marriage was neither a prerequisite of fully adult status nor a necessary condition of sexual experience. Margaret Mead contrasted the Samoan condition with that often found in Pacific communities: 'In many parts of the South Seas contact with white civilization has resulted in the complete degeneration of native life, the loss

[1] R. Firth, *Social Change in Tikopia* (1959), p. 46.

of native techniques and traditions, and the annihilation of the past. In Samoa this is not so.'[1]

The Tallensi of Ghana provide a final example of the integration of the young and social stability and conservatism which seem to be closely associated with it. Although the Tallensi desire some of the material products of Western civilization, and are prepared, as migrant labourers, to work for them, they 'still preserve the culture bequeathed to them by their forefathers and the social structure of their own, homogeneous society.'[2]

The Tallensi are a 'segmentary' and extremely egalitarian society, although they enjoin respect for age and seniority. But the young do not enter institutionalized age-groups with concerns distinct from those of their elders: 'the social sphere of adult and child is unitary and undivided.'[3] Children and adolescents share in the work of their elders as they are able; they have in consequence a sense of social purpose and importance, and of rights to which they are properly entitled. Young people learn their social and economic roles from close association with their parents or older siblings. 'The child is from the beginning oriented towards the same reality as its parents . . . The interests, motives and purposes of children are identical with those of adults, but at a simpler level of organization. Hence the children need not be coerced to take a share in economic and social activities. They are eager to do so.'

The Tallensi have resisted fundamental changes in their social system. Even the returning labourer-migrants, bringing back foreign ideas and exotic information, 'have made no appreciable impression on the native scheme of values and beliefs, or in their practical knowledge . . . Though they are one of the influences modifying the strict letter of custom in minor respects, they are not a disintegrating ferment in the native social order.'[4]

It is the contention of this chapter that such social resilience, conservatism and stability are directly causally related to the status and importance accorded to adolescents and young adults. There are undoubtedly circumstances in which a society with 'integrated' youth may succumb to, or even readily accept,

[1] Margaret Mead, *Coming of Age in Samoa* (Pelican Books 1954), p. 216.
[2] Myer Fortes, *The Dynamics of Clanship among the Tallensi* (1945), p. 12.
[3] Meyer Fortes, *Social and Psychological Aspects of Education in Taleland* (1938), p. 8.
[4] *The Dynamics of Clanship among the Tallensi* (1945), p. 11.

profound social change. The Ovimbundu of Angola may be such a people. Childs has described how, from later childhood, boys and girls assume a definite role in the work of the adult community. A boy at this age may make his first trip with a trading caravan, and will help his father in the fields. From the period of later childhood an Ovimbundu is a responsible person: he assumes considerable, and growing, economic responsibility, and is accounted legally responsible for his actions.[1]

More recent studies have shown profound changes in Umbundu society. The position of the Ovimbundu as traders and their deep involvement in the economic life of Europeans may be important factors in 'the very rapid social change'[2] that has occurred. But the change does not appear to be a vigorous and vital response to new opportunities: 'The present Umbundu social system deprived of any form of public life ticks over, as a man who has been paralysed may continue to live.'[3]

Segregation with Low Status

Segregated age-group institutions do not necessarily confer high status on the young or promise certain progress towards it. They may, on the contrary, signalize the rejection of the young from the central concerns of a society, underline their inferior standing, suggest their futility, and direct their attention to matters irrelevant to the major pre-occupations of the adult world. Such age-groups will be potentially deviant or at least experimental in new social forms which may provide an escape from the blockages from which their members suffer.[4]

Among the Tiv of Nigeria age-mates formerly constituted a mutual aid society for (largely ineffectual) protection against their

[1] See G. M. Childs, *Umbundu Kinship and Character* (1949).
[2] A. C. Edwards, *The Ovimbundu under Two Sovereignties* (1962), p. 155.
[3] Ibid., p. 160.
[4] Eisenstadt has argued that such potentially deviant age-groups, which do not function as mechanisms of social integration, are likely to arise in 'familistic societies': it is one of his major hypotheses that 'Age groups tend to arise when the structure of the family or descent group blocks the younger members' opportunities for attaining social status within the family (a) because the older members block the younger ones' access to the facilities which are prerequisites of full adult roles, and/or (b) the sharpening of incest taboos and restrictions on sexual relations within the family unit postpones the younger members' attainment of sexual maturity': op. cit., p. 248.

elders, particularly fathers and senior brothers. The latter possessed *tsav* by virtue of their age: supernatural power which ensured potency and skill, and was augmented by eating human flesh. The victim was provided by some other person, and the man who ate the flesh incurred a 'flesh-debt' which could be discharged only by supplying a close relative as an exchange victim.

Elders rich in *tsav* were consequently a serious menace to their younger kin. They were also powerful through their control over their sons' possibilities of marriage. Fully adult status was impossible until a man was married; but marriage could take place only when his father (or older married brother) supplied him with one of his daughters to give in exchange for a bride. The institution of exchange marriage placed a young man's advance to adult status at the caprice of his elders.

The younger Tiv had always been noted for their willingness for social experimentation, but the possibilities for this in the traditional society were limited. In 1927 an edict of the colonial government forbade exchange marriage and at a blow opened the floodgates of social change. The edict was resisted by the old, since it undermined the very basis of their power. But the young accepted it with eagerness, 'in fact these had been consulted and had been enthusiastically in its favour.'[1] Change now 'ramified in every aspect of the culture'. Freed from the tyranny of the old, young men fortified their position by working for wages in railway developments and other European enterprises. Henceforth, 'A man could get a wife through his own efforts, without waiting his turn, which depended on the priority of claims within the group, and without dependence on his father.'

Still more dramatic was the social change among the Manus of New Guinea in the interval between Margaret Mead's original study of them in the nineteen-twenties and her return visit twenty-five years later. The sheer weight of the Western impact, particularly in the shape of the American Army, must be held largely responsible for the fact that the Manus are 'a people who have moved faster than any people of whom we have records, a people who have moved in fifty years from darkest savagery to the twentieth century, men who have skipped over thousands of years of history in just the last twenty-five . . .'[2]

---

[1] See Margaret Mead (ed.), *Cultural Patterns and Technical Change* (1953), pp. 114–43.
[2] Margaret Mead, *New Lives for Old* (1956), p. 8.

A money economy has become established among the Manus, the clothing and calendar of the West, American-type marriage 'for love'. Old 'avoidances' (for example of mothers-in-law) have disappeared. But most significant of all, the position of the young in Manus society has changed, their importance has increased through Western education and more direct involvement in adult affairs. The sullen, aggressive, and brittle human relationships of the past seemed to have been generally superseded by easy and harmonious social intercourse.

Change had not been accepted with reluctance: 'the great avidity with which they seized on new situations'[1] had been the striking feature of their response to the massive contact of the West. In their traditional society the young had constituted an outsider group: trained in physical skills, prudery and respect for property, they were otherwise left to their own devices. Manus society was characterized by the cultural non-participation of the young, marked cultural discontinuity between the generations. 'There is no attempt to induct the child into this alien adult world,' wrote Margaret Mead in 1928. 'He is given no place in it and no responsibilities.'[2] 'Manus children live in a world of their own, a world from which adults are wilfully excluded, a world based on different premises from those of adult life.'[3] The result was latent deviance and a marked predisposition to seek in a new way of life personal significance unattainable in the old.

Rewards and Penalties

Latent deviance is likely to become actual when the rewards of change are sufficiently attractive, when they promise a real solution to the status difficulties of the young. (If the high rewards for the new behaviour continue, *further* change is likely to be impeded.) Similar educational techniques aimed specifically at fundamental culture-change will have widely different results if the social rewards of change are markedly different. It has commonly been observed that a new member of an organization,

[1] Ibid., p. 158.
[2] Margaret Mead, *Growing up in New Guinea* (Pelican Books 1942), p. 78.
[3] Ibid., p. 66.

society, or nation learns the new behaviour required of him more rapidly if he enjoys, or is promised, a position of high status; if his position is more lowly, although he is exposed to similar influences, he is more likely to cling to his former attitudes, values and customs. New recruits to the armed services, business institutions, neighbourhoods, more readily learn the speech idioms, methods of deportment and characteristic modes of behaviour, when they have success in the society's activities and are rewarded with enhanced prestige and formal standing. There is considerable evidence from American studies of immigrants that those who are rewarded with high status positions quickly become 'acculturated'; those of lower occupational rank cling more tenaciously to their former style of life (and tend, where possible, to occupy the same residential areas). If social change is to be effectively promoted among immigrants, they must be offered suitable rewards in the new system. As an American sociologist has recently concluded: 'if we are interested in acculturating immigrants to the United States, our social structure must be sufficiently open to offer them upward occupational mobility.'[1]

One of the most striking contrasts in the history of social change is that between the response of the Dakota Indians and the Janissaries of the Ottoman Empire to essentially similar methods of (forcible) 're-education'. The resounding success in the case of the latter and the dismal failure in the case of the former, are intelligible in terms of the social penalties and rewards attendant on the 'new learning'.

The remarkable educational institutions of the Ottoman Turks, in which Christian slaves, the 'Tribute of Blood', were prepared for the work of defending, extending, and ruling the domains of their masters, are not only among the most spectacular, but the most successful, in the history of education. For at least two centuries after the Turks captured Constantinople in 1453, slaves taken from the 'familistic' peasant societies of Greece, Albania, Serbia, Bosnia and Bulgaria, were successfully inducted

---

[1] S. Alexander Weinstock, 'Role Elements: A Link between Acculturation and Occupational Status', *British Journal of Sociology* (1963), 14. It is also the case that the role which goes with high occupational status spills over into wider areas of life, only marginally connected with work, than is commonly the case with a more lowly occupation. A wider area of life is necessarily changed for the immigrant corporation lawyer than for the doorman.

into the Mohammedan culture which they triumphantly carried half way to Dover.

The sons of shepherds and herdsmen were taken from their Greek Orthodox homes and trained to rule an Islamic Empire. Every boy was aware that he was a potential Grand Vizier. 'The Ottoman system deliberately took slaves and made them ministers of state. It took boys from the sheep-run and the plough-tail and made them courtiers and the husbands of princesses; it took young men whose ancestors had borne the Christian name for centuries, and made them rulers of the greatest Muhammedan states, and soldiers and generals in invincible armies whose chief joy was to beat down the Crown and elevate the Crescent . . .'[1]

The Christians were not taken as young children but at or a little before puberty, between the age of 10 and 14. They had learned one way of life and must now learn another. They had every inducement to do so. Their material needs were well cared for: the commanding officer of a battalion was the 'Soup Maker', the second-in-command the 'Head Water Carrier'; the regimental colours were the soup cauldron itself.

The majority were destined for a military career in which the top command positions were open to them. A carefully selected minority were embarked on a 14-year course of training and education, with rigorous weeding out along the route, for posts in the civil administration. The best entered the Palace School of the Grand Seraglio (there were usually some 300 pages, 600 during the reign of Soleyman the Magnificent in the sixteenth century). Three auxiliary schools (and later a fourth) each contained a similar number.

Those who passed with distinction through the first six or eight years of the course entered upon more specialized training in the Hall of the Expeditionary Force, the Hall of the Commissariat, the Hall of the Treasury, or the Hall of the Bedchamber. The liberal arts, the arts of government and of war, were the

---

[1] See H. H. Lybyer, *The Government of the Ottoman Empire at the Time of Soleyman the Magnificent* (1913). Cf. the sentimental and psychologically unreal version of H. A. L. Fisher, *A History of Europe* (1936), p. 402: 'The Janissary was a slave. The affections which sweeten the character, the interests which expand the mind, the ideals which give elevation to the will, were denied him. An iron discipline effaced the past and impoverished the future . . . he went forth to slay the enemies of the Sultan and of Allah with the inflamed and contracted fanaticism of a monk.'

subjects studied under notable scholars, mathematicians, and musicians who enjoyed royal patronage. Though technically 'slaves', and debarred from handing on wealth or position to their children, they had social and political eminence. Out of 60 Grand Viziers who have been traced in Turkish history, 48 were trained at the Palace School (the remaining 12, slaves also, started less promisingly in the artisan schools).[1]

Machiavelli and the Imperial Ambassador to Constantinople in the mid-sixteenth century have left contemporary testimony to the success of the system, to the stability and durability of a social and political order which, in the high prestige and power which it gave to young warriors and administrators, albeit of alien origin, had a built-in safeguard against deviation. (It was only with the establishment of hereditary offices in the civil and military hierarchies that the system failed to work effectively after the seventeenth century. The revolutionary 'Young Turks' of the twentieth century were the outcome of an increasingly closed and rigid social system.)

Machiavelli had offered no hope of internal support to the would-be invader of the Turkish state. He could not 'expect his enterprise to be aided by the defection of those whom the sovereign has around him . . . Whosoever, therefore, attacks the Turk must reckon on finding a united people . . .' Attacks against the kingdoms of Western Europe were much more hopeful 'since you will always find in them men who are discontented and desirous of change . . .'[2]

Busbecq, who was Imperial Ambassador to Constantinople intermittently between 1555 and 1562 analysed this stability and high morale in greater detail: 'No distinction is attached to birth among the Turks; the deference to be paid to a man is measured by the position he holds in the public service . . . honours, high posts and judgeships are the rewards of great ability and good service. If a man be dishonest, or lazy, or careless, he remains at the bottom of the ladder, an object of contempt, for such qualities there are no honours in Turkey. This is the reason that they are successful in their undertakings, that they lord it over others, and are daily extending the bounds of their empire. These are not our (European) ideas; with us there is no opening left for merit;

[1] See Barnette Miller, *The Palace School of Muhammad the Conqueror* (1941), pp. 6–7.
[2] N. Machiavelli, *The Prince*, trans. N. H. Thomson (1913), Bk. 4, pp. 24–5.

birth is the standard for everything; the prestige of birth is the sole key to advancement in the public service.'[1]

The Federal authorities of America attempted, in the later-nineteenth and early-twentieth centuries, to induct the youth of the Indian tribes into the culture of white America. Their methods—enforced and prolonged schooling of the young away from their parents, an 'immensely thoughtful and costly experiment in federal Indian education'[2]—nowhere met with the resounding success of the remarkably similar institutions of the Ottoman Turks, and often with pathetic failure. This was not because the American soldiers, administrators, and educators lacked the thoroughness, ruthlessness, resources or pedagogical skills of the Turks in the days of Soleyman the Magnificent. The Indian children had learned one culture; they refused to learn another. Whereas the Turks offered boundless social rewards for social change and new learning, the Americans offered not top command posts in the army, civil administration and business corporations; but only life as marginal men and second-class citizens on the reserves.

There were some tribes for whom even this was an escape from the social blockages and frustrations of the indigenous order. Thus the Makah, formerly characterized by rigid social stratification, were more successfully assimilated than most: as fishermen they found rewards in the prosperity of wider American markets. And re-education was ruthless: 'Parents who refused to send their children to school were imprisoned until they saw the uselessness of refusal.'[3] But a similar technique and equal ruthlessness left the once vigorous and self-confident Dakota only apathetic, listlessly discarding the new values and customs they were taught.

The proud and virile Dakota had hunted buffalo across the prairie: an egalitarian society, 'a hunter democracy, levelling every potential dictator and every potential capitalist.'[4] The young male was accorded prestige and importance. 'Every educational device was used (by the Dakota) to develop in the boy a maximum of self-confidence . . . He was to become a

[1] Quoted C. T. Forster and F. H. B. Daniell, *The Life and Letters of Ogier Ghiselin de Busbecq* (1881), vol. 1, pp. 152–5.
[2] Erik H. Erikson, *Childhood and Society* (1951), p. 98.
[3] Elizabeth Colson, op. cit., p. 20.
[4] E. H. Erikson, op. cit., p. 101.

hunter after game, woman and spirit.' In his upbringing, emphasis was placed on 'his right to autonomy and on his duty of initiative.'[1] The federal authorities aimed to bring about change to the American way of life through systematic teaching. 'Children were virtually kidnapped to force them into government schools, their hair was cut and their Indian clothes thrown away. They were forbidden to speak in their own language . . . Parents who objected were also jailed. Where possible, children were kept in school year after year to avoid the influence of their families.'[2] These measures failed. The American cowboy culture was an inadequate recompense for the lost satisfactions of a vanished tribal life.

The Best of Both Worlds

Poised between the old world and the new, the young in non-literate tribal societies have often been able to use the new world to perpetuate the old. Savings from wages earned as migrant labourers have enabled them to return to their traditional societies not to change them, but to secure with their wealth a valued status within the traditional framework. They have a sociological significance not unlike that of the eighteenth-century nabobs who returned from India to buy positions in English society which, in the majority of cases could not have been theirs if they had remained at home. Far from aiming to transform the society to which they returned after exotic experiences abroad, they attained significance precisely by supporting the social structure which gave them the chance to buy a place in the squirearchy, the exclusive clubs, and the most expensive and exclusive of them all, the House of Commons.

Inevitably the enriched tribesman changes his society to some extent when he returns. He belongs to a class of *nouveaux riches* which threatens established political and social authorities. He enjoys independence of paternal (and avuncular) authority. And yet if such men desire status in terms of the social order in which they grew up, they will seek to preserve it, to minimize the effect that they themselves have upon it. There is no gain in buying

[1] Ibid., p. 128.
[2] See G. MacGregor, op. cit.

one's way into an aristocracy which has been undermined and is in a state of decay.

Young men of the Tonga tribe on the shores of Lake Nyasa regard it as normal to spend some part of their early lives working in the Rhodesias or South Africa. 'Young men consider their stay in the village, before they go off to the towns, as a period of marking time.'[1] But even while they are away, they manoeuvre for office and position within the traditional social structure. They are concerned to maintain the traditional values and social order, and 'when they return from an urban life abroad they settle again in the pattern of Tonga life which is still dominated by traditional values. There are no obvious signs of social disorganization and the Tonga still hold together as a tribal unit distinct from other such units around them.'

Similarly with the Tikopia and the Tallensi. The young men of Tikopia who go abroad to work retain their rights and interests in the homeland. Though clearly they are a potential threat to established authorities when they return with comparative wealth, they seek not to overthrow traditional authorities but to enter into alliance with them. By the late nineteen-thirties the young men of Taleland were also leaving home in large numbers to work elsewhere for wages. But 'labour migrants remain strongly attached to their families and natal settlements, and it is always assumed that they will eventually return . . . and when they do return they resume the traditional way of life.'[2]

The *nouveaux riches* among the Ngoni have used the wealth they earned in European work to buy social status in traditional terms. They have converted cash into cows. If they were formerly cultivators, without cattle, the mere possession of cows will not in itself bring high social status. 'But if he goes with due deference to the older men who own cattle to ask for advice and technical help about building his kraal and breeding in his herd, in course of time they will include him in their discussions about cattle when they sit in the men's talking place.'[3] But what he cannot do for himself he can do for his sons. His cattle can secure them well-connected brides, and his grandchildren at least will be

[1] See J. Van Velsen, 'Labour Migration as a Positive Factor in the Continuity of Tonga Tribal Society', in A. Southall, op. cit.
[2] Meyer Fortes, *The Dynamics of Clanship among the Tallensi* (1945), p. 11.
[3] Margaret Read, *Native Standards of Living and African Culture Change* (1938), p. 32.

assured of the highest social standing through the dignity of birth on the mother's side. Social change is impeded by contact with the West.

In all these instances young men had a position of some importance or significance even in the 'pre-contact' social order; they were not potential deviants looking for an escape from their frustrations in the opportunities of a new civilization. The new civilization has enabled them to become even more important in traditional terms; they are even less inclined to deviate from old standards, customs and values. It may be one of the ironies of the human condition that any society must choose between social conservatism and rigidity, or the oppression of its young.

Chapter Eight

YOUTH AND THE FUTURE

A Handicapped Élite

IN adolescence the young attain physical maturity, the height of their sexual powers,[1] the peak of intellectual capacity.[2] These attributes are susceptible to measurement; and while the 'spread' may be wide—some adolescents will achieve physical, sexual and intellectual maturity some years before others—the culmination of development in these respects during adolescence is open to verification. Those adults who would not dispute this may yet maintain that at 16, 17, or 18, young people are far from maturity—they are lacking in 'wisdom'. It is fortunate for their case that wisdom has no generally agreed definition, cannot be measured, and its distribution established.

However 'mature' adolescents may in reality be, a small minority must be prepared to accept a position of dependence and tutelage while they remain in educational institutions until their twenties to acquire the skills and knowledge which a highly developed industrial civilization requires. Their sacrifices: their postponement of manhood, the stresses and conflicts to which they are subjected, should not be underrated; nor should their numbers be unnecessarily swollen. For the multiplication of

---

[1] See A. C. Kinsey et al., *Sexual Behaviour in the Human Male* (1948). 'The maximum sexual frequencies (total outlet) occur in the teens'. 'It is probable that in a population which married at an earlier age, the highest frequency on the curve would come in the earlier adolescent group; but in our society as it is, the high point of sexual performance (for males) is, in actuality, somewhere around 16 or 17 years of age' (p. 219).

[2] See P. E. Vernon, *Intelligence and Attainment* (1960). 'The growth of intelligence seems to slow down soon after 12 years and to cease somewhere around 14 to 16 years (this statement too will require later qualification)' (p. 11), and 'average adult test scores are no higher than those of 13–16 year olds' (p. 15). However there is some evidence that 'growth continues as long as education or other intellectually stimulating conditions continue, though probably never beyond about 25–30 years, and that when such stimulation ceases a decline sets in' (pp. 152–4).

higher qualifications does not necessarily mean the multiplication of senior and demanding jobs: the job may remain the same, but the qualifications asked for, amidst an abundance of the qualified, may be ever higher. A relatively 'unqualified' man may have done the same job with competence, even distinction, twenty or fifty years ago. As higher education expands, work for which a School Certificate was formerly an adequate preparation, may now require a higher degree.

In some callings, perhaps particularly those involving skill in human relationships (as opposed to science and technology), a prolonged education may reduce rather than enhance a person's competence. It is doubtful whether prolonged study of the social sciences or of the humanities affords an adequate substitute for experience. (The Cornell Values Survey of 1952 in 11 American universities did not find the social values of social science students different from those of other students such as engineers. In fact little difference in values seemed to be promoted by different subject specialisms.) A segregated life with selected coevals similar in abilities, background and values is not the ideal preparation for men of affairs. Yet 'managers', in the broadest sense, must be drawn from their numbers, since, with the refinement of selection techniques, those who entered life earlier are unlikely to have the necessary native intelligence—though they may well have many other most valuable attributes of personality—to cope satisfactorily with the more formal problem-solving aspects of the job.

Our institutions of higher learning are necessary for those who require training for advanced specialisms; they can provide an effective training, but ever less an education in the sense of encouraging the pursuit of truth for its own sake, the enjoyment of intellectual activity for its intrinsic excitement, the cultivation of the mind and sensibilities. The promotion of 'intellectual excellence' which Newman so eloquently advocated, or of 'good states of mind' no less eloquently recommended by Clive Bell,[1] has been ever less possible as education has become a major instrument of social engineering. It would be ludicrous to suggest that the blinkered application required of undergraduates today produced civilized men and women as either Bell or New-

[1] See Clive Bell, *Civilisation* (1928). The civilized man 'will value art and thought and knowledge for their own sakes, not for their possible utility'; he will, above all, cultivate 'good states of mind'.

man understood the term. It produces experts. (But all history
graduates cannot become professional historians; they remain all
too often, as salesmen or civil servants, historians manqués.)
Occasionally, by accident or by default, civilized men and women
may be produced. But this has been ever less likely since education
became the determinant rather than the accompaniment of social
status. An education fit for gentlemen was unlikely to survive
when there were no gentlemen left.[1] There is even a sense of
unreality in discussing education in the terms of Bell or Newman;
Fred Clarke and Mannheim have since shown us new perspectives.
We are all sociologists now.[2]

Those who do not attend our institutions of higher education
may fail to attain the highest social and economic rewards; but
they do not necessarily, if we use our society aright, fail to
receive an education. Valuable educational opportunities exist,
and could be more extensively and attractively provided, after
formal education is completed—for many, the best time for
education to begin. While a true education, the cultivation of the
mind for its own sake, is ever less available in the grammar
schools, the colleges of advanced technology and the universities,
it is readily available in the courses run by the W.E.A. and the
university departments of adult education. These are the last
strongholds of learning pursued for its own sake, offering no
promise of social and vocational advancement, granting no
certificates. The proper use of wireless and television could
make such courses still more widely available. It is the essence of
such educational activities that they are voluntarily undertaken
by adults interested in the study of a body of knowledge and
ideas for its own sake. The definition of 'adult' needs to be more

[1] J. H. Newman, *The Idea of a University* (1929) edition, Discourse V: 'Liberal
education makes not the Christian, not the Catholic, but the gentleman. It is well to
be a gentleman, it is well to have a cultivated intellect, a delicate taste, a candid,
equitable, dispassionate mind, a noble and courteous bearing in the conduct of
life . . .'
[2] Whatever may be the validity of a university's claims to promote intellectual skills,
extensive and technically sophisticated American research should make us cautious
in expecting a modern university education invariably or even commonly to promote
more than a superficial change in values: 'the value changes which seem to occur in
college and set the college alumnus apart from others are not very great, at least for
most students at most institutions. They certainly do not support the widely held
assumption that a college education has an important, general, almost certain
"liberalizing" effect' (F. E. Jacob, op. cit., p. 50). But of course it is time we did our
own research into these matters.

generous—to include 16-year-olds on equal terms, and not as a special and limited 'student' membership. And doubtless such study will always be a minority pursuit; the disinterested search for enlightenment is always likely to be.

Those who enter upon formal courses of higher education need not be so severely handicapped and penalized as they tend to be today. The gifted minority who follow courses of academic and professional study from 11 to their mid- (or late-) twenties, need not be so dependent, humiliated, excluded from the life of their society, as commonly they are at present. University students should be regarded as junior members of the academic staff (an old but fast disappearing ideal of the ancient universities), and appropriately salaried, as colleagues rather than a separate race dependent on charitable doles. And adequate accommodation should be provided for those who wish to marry. Theoretical continence, and even more so actual continence, is a savage price exacted from the young at the height of their physical powers for the benefits of higher learning.

But most important is the need to question the sanctity of the residential principle in institutions of higher education. The *educational* virtues of residential schools and colleges have only recently been claimed. For long it seemed obvious that residence might be a necessary evil: at the best it would promote undue gregariousness, at the worst unmentionable vice. The educative properties of peer groups have relatively recently been brought to our notice. The ancient public schools and universities became residential chiefly for disciplinary purposes: when students were scattered in private houses in the town the authority of the head master or college head was circumscribed. The higher virtues of residence were not self-evident to later-nineteenth-century educationists. When the new teacher training colleges of the nineteenth century were established on residential lines, the Report of the Newcastle Commission on Elementary Education (1861) deplored the immaturity which was bred in their students. The *day* training colleges—the precursors of university departments of education—were established in the universities after 1890 as a matter of principle, and not as a means of providing a university education for intending teachers on the cheap. The college hostel is an excellent device designed to keep men boys.

In the mid-twentieth century only Balogh's lonely voice has

questioned the sacrosanct status of university residence. He concedes that for purely practical reasons student hotels (not hostels or pseudo-colleges) might be necessary to provide accommodation for undergraduates; but argues that these should not contain only students. Young professional people and students at technical colleges would live there too. He rejects outright the current ideal which demands 'the isolation at all costs of the young men and women in the new universities from the murky reality of urban life in industrial England', the notion that 'they should be housed not as adults, mixing with other people from all walks of life, but separately in small colleges *in statu pupillari*'.[1]

The re-integration of students with society is an urgent need not only for their own sanity and mature development (and proper sense of social values), but for their greater effectiveness when eventually they take up their careers. The unreality of contemporary student life, its apartness, its lack of immediate social relevance and sense of usefully contributing to the nation's concerns, are causes of stress and conflict which can without great difficulty, and even with considerable economy, be eradicated.

The Threatened Majority

Even the 'unselected', allegedly underprivileged, majority, who leave school at 15 or 16, are ever more treated as a separate race to be confined in appropriately juvenile institutions. At work they are increasingly classified and underpaid as 'apprentices' when in fact they do a man's job (though some forms of apprenticeship are undoubtedly necessary and valuable); in leisure the attempt is made to herd them into spaces insulated from all contact with adult concerns.

The Albermarle Report on the Youth Service in England and Wales[2] is one of the most disastrous social documents to appear in this country this century. It widens the fissure in English society which divides the generations and, no doubt with the best

---

[1] T. Balogh, 'Universities or Sixth Forms', *Times Educational Supplement* (30 November 1962), p. 711.
[2] *The Youth Service in England and Wales* (1960): Report of the Committee Appointed by the Ministry of Education.

intentions in the world, belittles and humiliates the young. It advocates that there be established a separate, segregated, adolescent world (for young people between 14 and 20) with specially trained (and paid) representatives of adult society to supervise and oversee it. In spite of the Report's elaborate parade of sympathy for adolescence, it offers the firm reproof: 'Young people are greedy for adult status, and some of them anticipate it'. There is, throughout the Report, no conception of introducing young people into adult institutions, even as junior members. Even the political activities of the young, if any, should be essentially the politics of youth: speakers should themselves be young, and not members of older generations.

Two threats which appeared in the Education Act of 1944 have not yet been implemented: that the minimum school leaving age be raised to 16, and that there be compulsory attendance at County Colleges for those who have left school but are not yet 18 years of age. These proposals have received further support from the Crowther Report (1959). As the employment of the swollen numbers of adolescents becomes more difficult, both these recommendations are quite certain, after a quarter of a century, to be put into effect.

There is no justification on educational grounds for making 16 the statutory minimum leaving age. There can be no justification for prolonging by yet another year the kind of experience which Mays, for instance, very soberly describes in inner-urban secondary-modern schools—and Mays himself is very dubious about the wisdom of such a prolongation: 'If we could choose between a better and more successful education up to 15 for the down-town boys and girls or another year spent in existing conditions, there is no doubt that the former policy should prevail.'[1]

If we are genuinely concerned with the psychological and social welfare of the young, for some at least the school leaving age should be lowered—perhaps even for a majority of secondary-modern school children. There is no justification in either psychology or biology for requiring the same minimum leaving age for all children (or, for that matter, the same age for entry into universities and professional courses of training). The change from school to work, further education or the university should

[1] J. B. Mays, op. cit., p. 200.

be made in the light of the individual's physical development, emotional needs, social maturity, manual capacity, and intelligence.

Tanner has suggested that a boy might spend a considerable part of his time in an engineering workshop or other employment from the age of 13.[1] Because child labour was once 'exploited' in this country, it does not follow that, with due safeguards erected in the light of history, the same would happen again. It is probably still true that adults are not to be trusted, that we cannot confidently expect them voluntarily to behave with decency and humanity towards the young; but we now have social and legal machinery, and can provide more, to make them do so.

The 12- or 13-year-old who was in part-time work would still be the responsibility of the local education authorities. The decision that he should go to work would be arrived at after assessment of his attitudes, aptitudes and abilities by the education authorities and consultation with the boy or girl and the parents. The Leicestershire Experiment trusts parents with the decision to keep their children on at school after 15; it may be that parents are sufficiently responsible to be allowed some say in taking their children away before. So that their decision should not be too difficult, all children after the age of 13, whether at school or at work, should be in receipt of an income, paid either from public funds, like family allowances (but paid to the young person direct), or by industry if he were employed.

County colleges, like youth clubs, are an agency for manufacturing adolescents where none naturally exist. Like apprenticeship they are justified only when they genuinely enhance the status of youth, make them capable of realizing their full potential, able to hold their own with, and perhaps often to surpass, adults both socially and economically. To the extent that they segregate the young, *make* them a distinct population with separate interests and concerns, underline their status as learners, they are to be deplored. To introduce compulsory attendance would be an intolerable affront, direction of labour and infringement of personal liberty without justification in our social and political philosophy—except on the assumption that we are dealing with people who are in fact less than persons.

[1] J. M. Tanner, *Education and Physical Growth* (1961), p. 124.

In the colleges which have already started young people have valued the time they have spent there when they were equipped with worthwhile technical and professional skills and recognized qualifications.[1] The idealists may lament that they did not generally seek in the county college opportunities for cultural development and 'personal enrichment'. It is a delusion to imagine that personal enrichment can in any case result from a day a week at a county college if the surrounding days are filled with frustration and humiliation. Personal enrichment is a function of a way of life: it will be achieved when the circumstances of home, work and leisure make possible a sense of personal worth and dignity.

The fissure which runs through our society and separates the adolescents from their seniors will not be bridged by attempting to make the young more comfortable on their side of the divide. Indeed, real comfort and self-respect are possible only when they move into the hostile camp and gain acceptance in its affairs.

There is a general need for lowering the age of admission into English social and cultural institutions, for taking in 16-year-olds and according them the rights, and imposing the responsibilities, which apply to their seniors. Political and legal maturity should be recognized at 17; the trend to more youthful marriage accepted and aided instead of deplored. (The surprising thing is not that some youthful marriages break down, but that so many survive in an atmosphere of disapproval and disparagement.) The sexual powers and needs of adolescents need frank recognition; heterosexual experience in adolescence must be accepted, instruction in birth-control given. (And if prostitution is driven underground and made an expensive luxury for, in the main, the middle-aged and married, we must expect that young men will make sexual demands upon their girl friends.) The contemporary social order and adult social attitudes are based, if not upon hypocrisy, on gigantic myths concerning the needs and nature of the young.

Young people must be provided not with separate, scaled-down versions of adult institutions, political, social and recreational, but admitted as junior partners into adult concerns: or as senior partners when they show their capacity to hold senior positions. After 14 or 15, age needs to become increasingly an irrelevance in judging an individual's worth. Too many erroneous inferences

[1] J. B. Mays, op. cit., p. 172.

are drawn from a person's accumulation—or lack of accumulation —of years.

Age Barriers in the School

Our schools breed an exaggerated respect for the often irrelevant criterion of age. Increasingly they have been organized and stratified according to precise distinctions of age. In the first half of the twentieth century the all-age school (and class) have appeared to educational theorists and administrators as self-evident obstacles to educational progress and efficiency. Elementary education after 1862, on the other hand, under the now infamous Revised Code, grouped children in 'standards' according to their attainments. Large schools, particularly under the 'Hadow' re-organization after 1926, made it possible to establish streams within a given year of age, to keep children of the same academic standard *and* of the same age together. We have given a new importance to age at the very time that we have been discovering its irrelevance. 'Age' is the first item of information asked for on any educational (or other personal) record card. The civilized, industrial societies differ sharply from the primitive in the precision with which they measure an individual's age and in the significance they attach to it.

Age may be a most misleading index of abilities. The notions of 'mental age' and of 'social age', which may differ considerably from chronological age, are a recognition of this. As the size of the scatter in individual growth patterns increases in adolescence, it is ever less a reliable index of physical, social, mental or emotional maturity. Age becomes ever more an irrelevant criterion of fitness to undertake a wide range of tasks and responsibilities. Its prime virtue is its administrative convenience. (Its irrelevance was finally recognized by the General Certificate of Education examination after the initial attempt to prevent anyone sitting the examination under the age of 16.)

Tanner has suggested 'skeletal age' as the most meaningful way of classifying the young. This provides a measure of 'general physiological status' and a more accurate pointer to the level of capacities and abilities. 'Because individuals vary so much in the age at which they reach adolescence, and because adolescence involves such relatively large changes in body size, physiological function and social behaviour, the bald statement that a boy is aged 14 is in most contexts hopelessly vague.'[1] If we wish to teach classes which are homogeneous (and some, of course, will advocate a measure of diversity), then we should select children of the same 'developmental age'. Both schools and society are likely to do greater justice by individuals and promote increased educational and social efficiency, if they look beyond chronological age and accord duties, responsibilities and rights in the light of actual capacities.

In general our adolescents are older than we think, our treatment of them barbarous and insulting. Attempts to treat them in ways appropriate to their real, or any way, potential level of development, have been few, and often with unrepresentative samples of children. Courageous attempts have been made in 'progressive' schools; and in the Leicestershire Plan there is at least the administrative provision for their more adult treatment. (But in the event, so much depends upon persons, upon the attitudes of teachers.)

The Mason Plan in Leicestershire has lopped off the pre-adolescents from the grammar schools in order that the 14- to 18-year-olds may be treated in a more adult fashion. But in general the maintained grammar schools have not been remarkable this century for their acceptance of such 'progressive' ideas—the ideas of Dewey, of Reddie, of Curry or of Neill. They have not responded to Dewey's arguments that the barriers between school and the surrounding world be lowered—they often remain remarkably aloof from the localities in which they are embedded[2] and their curricula are only tenuously related to the local world. Nor have they followed the progressives in lowering the barriers between teachers and pupils within their walls.

While some of our public schools today may approximate to the grammar schools in their staff-pupil relationships, 'progressivism' as developed at Abbotsholme and Dartington Hall grew out of the nineteenth-century public school tradition. It emphasized the corporate life of staff and students on equal or near-equal

---

[1] J. M. Tanner, *Physical Maturing and Growth at Adolescence* (1959), p. 29.
[2] Cf. 'School Rules and Class Attitudes in State Education', *The Guardian* (5 February 1963), p. 8: 'the grammar schools try to cut their pupils off from the local community, in which they might otherwise expect to be natural leaders. This cutting off is often the reason for compelling pupils to wear school uniform.'

terms. Student participation in school government—the exercise of real power by pupils—has been one of its salient features. This tradition is alien to the day grammar school. The strongest supporters of 'the grammar-school tradition' in the mid-twentieth century have tended to be anti-progressive and authoritarian.

The grammar schools have continued to place emphasis on disciplined learning rather than on creativity, on correct deport-ment (symbolized by the compulsory school uniform) rather than on spontaneity of behaviour. They commonly impose belittling restrictions upon their pupils which are justified as an attempt to maintain high standards of personal conduct. Recent inquiries in grammar schools led to the following conclusions: 'Grammar schools with socially and educationally ambitious head masters and others with a large working-class intake often regulate their pupils' activities in a way which is irrelevant to education . . . In furthering these (social and educational) ambitions they may be unaware that the rules they impose are unusually restrictive. It is odd, however, how evasive some head masters are about their rules.'[1] One head master even imposes a 7 o'clock curfew (9 o'clock at weekends) on his 18- and 19-year-old day boys.

It is probably a mistake to regard the orthodox grammar school as a (somewhat watered-down) version of the public school. Most grammar-school masters would find public-school boys offensive in their attitudes, intolerably 'familiar' (and more often their social equals or superiors). The state primary and modern schools are probably nearer today to the public schools in the personal relationships between teachers and taught which they practise and approve.

Profound modification of staff-pupil relationships in the maintained grammar schools is one of the most pressing educa-tional problems of our times—which can, perhaps, be most effectively tackled in the initial training of teachers. Boys and girls in the upper school (and there is a case for starting the Sixth Form, at least as a social classification, at the age of 15), must be treated with less hauteur than is now commonly the case—the boys might even be addressed as mister and the girls as miss.[2] A greater share in the government of the school, including

---

[1] Ibid.
[2] B. Jackson and D. Marsden, op. cit., similarly arguef or the treatment of grammar-school pupils as adults (pp. 202–5).

adequate representation at the staff meeting, might help to allay the self-disparagement, conflict and unhappiness which seem to characterize the grammar-school pupil today.

There has been an altogether unfortunate emphasis this century on the school as an institution catering for the supposedly 'characteristic needs' of adolescence. 'But before anything else,' maintained the Spens Report on Secondary Education (1939), the school should provide for the pre-adolescent and adolescent years a life which answers their special needs and brings out their special values'. This is disastrous advice. It creates a socio-psychological classification where none naturally exists; it *makes* young people 'adolescents', a psychologically distinct subsection of the race.

A more generous and accurate recognition of the real nature and potential of adolescents, their close approximation to adults, might lead to a population of young people less in conflict with themselves and with the world. It is possible that our society might in consequence lose some of its dynamic: without a frustrated younger generation it might lose some of its inventiveness. But the oppression of a section of our population for the sake of greater social drive can have no justification in ethics. A reduced degree of social innovation might be a price worth paying for a more relaxed, humane and just society. But there is no need to worry unduly on this score: the outlook for youth in the immediate future is such that they are likely to be goaded into far more activity and deviation than they have been for a quarter of a century.

Prospects for Youth

It is not possible to end this book on a note of hope. Demographic circumstances, economic conditions, educational strategy and provision, and the institutionalized power of adults make it unlikely that any of the changes in the treatment of the young which have been advocated above, will come about.

Biologically 'the young' of this book are ever older; but with varying measures of success powerful attempts are made to make them ever younger. Tanner has shown how, 'During the last hundred years there has been a very striking tendency for the time of adolescence to become earlier, and for the whole process of growth to be speeded up'.[1] The process is continuing. 'Menarche has been getting earlier by about four months per decade in Western Europe over the period 1840 to 1960. Thus a girl may expect to menstruate on average some ten months earlier than her mother did.'[2] And yet society has successfully made the adolescent *less* mature. The present-day 14-year-old is 'in physique and very probably brain maturity' equal to the 15-year-old of a generation ago. 'If his social behaviour seems less rather than more mature (in the sense here of adult-like) that must be laid at the door of the social and educational pressures bearing or failing to bear upon him.'[3]

As a society we have been astonishingly successful in ignoring biology.[4] Indeed, it is precisely as the maturity of the young has been accelerated, since the middle of last century, that we have kept them in ever longer tutelage and dependence. This is a tribute to the power of social institutions and the organization of the mature. Perhaps, indeed, they have been kept in ever longer subordination just because they are more mature and consequently threatening to the old. Whatever biological changes may have occurred over the past century, 'where society does not permit the adolescent to assume a social role compatible with his physical and intellectual development, but keeps him dependent and irresponsible at home, adult maturity is come by with more difficulty'.[5]

There is no good reason to suppose that the mature will change their strategy. Changes in our economy and in our population structure are on their side. An industrialist, Mr S. M. de Bartolomé, the Master Cutler, recently gave an accurate diagnosis of the predicament of the young in industry today:[6]

---

[1] J. M. Tanner, *Education and Physical Growth* (1961), p. 113.

[2] Ibid., p. 118.

[3] Ibid., p. 123.

[4] Tanner shows how tenuous is the connection between biology and the overt behaviour of adolescents: 'It has some times been thought that at adolescence an increase in physiological instability or day-to-day fluctuation in physiological functions occurs, due to the considerable changes taking place. The supposed existence of such a phase of development has even been said to condition the instability of psychological reactions at this time. In fact the only data capable of throwing light on this question show no evidence of any such increase in physiological instability.' See *Growth at Adolescence* (1962 edition), p. 157.

[5] Ibid., p. 218.

[6] 'Industrial Earnings in Reverse?': report of an address delivered in Sheffield, *The Guardian* (9 April 1963), p. 15.

the 'age pyramid' no longer exists; there is not a thinning out of senior people, with men getting scarcer as they get older. Senior men live longer; they are less likely, under our present system of taxation, to retire early. There are now far more younger men competing for senior and better paid jobs than has been the case in the past.

And yet, with the expansion of higher education, far more of the young men are well qualified for the senior posts which are now less quickly vacated. The young subordinate may be patently better equipped for the senior post than its relatively ill-educated, elderly incumbent—though the latter, it is true, will claim greater 'wisdom'. The senior and elderly, thinks Mr Bartolomé, must step aside for their younger colleagues, accept demotion and correspondingly reduced incomes. 'Logically,' he maintains, 'this must mean that a lot of middle-aged people, now in comfortable employment, will lose their jobs or have to take something worse paid.' He produces no evidence of any tendency for a less qualified but deeply entrenched older generation to step gracefully—or even reluctantly—aside in the interests of the numerous and highly qualified young. It is, indeed, the height of *naïveté* to suppose that in this matter, logic—or even humanity—will prevail.

INDEX

Index

Coevals
adolescents' attitudes towards, 95–6
contamination by, 39, 47
education by, 42, 51, 153
Colonial Service, 8
Comanche Indians, 134–5
Compleat English Gentleman, The, 36 n., 39 n., 48 n.
Concordance, coefficient of, 113–14
Conflict
between cultures, 126, 130–31
between generations, 2, 86–7, 100–105, 130–31, 140–42, 162–3
in grammar-school pupils, 108, 114–20
Conforming character type, 15
Continence as the price of a higher education, 153
County colleges
for manufacturing adolescents, 156–7
proposed, 155
Crowther Report, 122, 155
Cruelty to children, 58, 60 n., 62–3

DAY, THOMAS, 44 n., 50 n., 63
Death as an educational subject, 34
DEFOE, DANIEL, 35, 36, 39, 48
Delinquency, 20–21, 22, 34
Dependency, training for in pre-adolescence, 16
Depression among adults and adolescents, 14
Deviance, latent, 21, 107, 131, 142, 161
Discipline, alleged need for, 61, 102
Domestic education, 37–46
Dress in adolescence, 11, 33, 101, 102

Earnings of young people, 67, 68, 71, 84
EDGEWORTH, RICHARD LOVELL, 36 n., 40 n., 44, 46, 48, 61, 63
Education
adult, 152
and values, 9, 151, 152, 154
as ritual, 23, 28
compulsory, 73, 74, 75
for experts, 151–2
for gentlemen, 152
prolongation of, 23, 24, 25, 26, 28, 81, 82, 155
tribal, 6, 26, 27, 28
for women, 50–51
within the family, 37–46
Education Acts, 58, 59, 74, 81
Émile, 33 n., 42, 52 n., 62 n., 64 n.
Employment of youth
contemporary trends, 7–8, 19–20, 21, 23–4, 82–5, 151, 156, 163
nineteenth century, 66–76
Expedient character type, 15
Experts, 152, 157
Extraversion, 4–9

Factory Acts, 34, 58, 73, 74
Factory girls, 67, 68, 77, 78
Family
influence on life-chances, 28–32
in America, 87, 88, 103, 104
in France, 36, 59, 87
education within, 37–46
power within, 10, 60 n., 67, 68, 79, 137, 141
size, 59, 60, 65, 73
Fantasies in adolescence, 14, 18–19
Fathers
adolescents' attitudes towards, 87, 88, 97–100, 116
as dependants, 67
as tutors, 39–46, 68–9
France
adolescent peer groups, 87
family life, 36, 59–60, 87
opportunities for youth, 66
Revolutionary influences, 61
FROMM, ERICH, 83
Frustrations of youth, 3, 28, 50, 83, 106, 126–7, 129, 140–42, 153, 161–3

Gerontocracy, 24
GODWIN, WILLIAM, 40
Grammar schools
as ordeal, 28
authoritarian traditions, 4, 160
'democratic', 32
pupils
aspirations, 31
conflicts, 4, 9, 25, 108, 114–20
immaturity, 25
leisure activities, 122–3
negative attitudes, 109–10
orthodoxy, 106–7
staff-student relationships, 123–4, 159, 160
unlike public schools, 160

HALL, STANLEY, 56
Halls of residence in universities, 153–4
'Hardening', 62–3
HARTLEY, DAVID, 40
Hatred of the mature for the young, 10, 101–2, 156
HELVETIUS, 40, 41, 42
Hazelwood school, 46
High schools, American, 26, 29–31
HOGGART, RICHARD, 25, 106, 108

Innate characteristics (18th century view), 40–42
Inoculation (18th century), 62
Insurance as a substitute for children, 71–2
Intelligence of adolescents, 150

Index

Promotion
  prospects for the young (19th century), 66
  prospects today, 21, 84, 163
Prostitution, 157
Puberty, age of, 161–2
Public Schools
  as age-grade organizations (18th century), 47, 49
  as a last resort, 46, 48
  changing function, 49–50
  status conferred by, 49, 57
  riots at, 48–9
  personal relations in, 159–60

Radley College, 55
Rational-altruistic character, 15
Realism of youth, 17–18, 23
Research, need for, 7 n., 9 n., 14, 104, 152 n.
Responsibility, adolescents' sense of, 22, 95–6
RIESMAN, DAVID, 86, 111
Riots
  among apprentices, 48
  at public schools, 48–9
Role, adolescent
  adult conception of, 11–13, 101–2
  conflict, 114–20
  training for, 13–14, 16–17
ROUSSEAU, JEAN-JACQUES, 33, 42, 44, 52, 53, 56, 62, 64
RUSSELL, BERTRAND, 54

Samoans, 137, 138–9
School leaving age, see age of school leaving
Schools, see grammar schools, modern schools, public schools
Segmentary tribes, position of youth, 132–5, 137, 139
Self-image of adolescents, 95–6
Servility
  of grammar-school pupils, 4, 23, 106
  of public school boys (18th century), 47
  of undergraduates, 21–2
Sexuality in adolescence, 150, 153, 157
Social change
  forced, 128, 135
  and migration, 147–9
  and social rewards, 142–7
  and status frustration, 46–7, 126, 129, 131–2, 140–42

Social-class differences
  in adults' attitudes to adolescents, 101
  in adolescents' attitudes to school, 109
  in role-conflict, 116
Social competence in adolescence, 16, 95–6, 162
Social distance between age groups, 36–7, 94–5
SOUTHEY, ROBERT, 42, 63
Status (of the young)
  and marriage, 58, 77, 79, 80, 81, 132, 141
  and employment, 65–8, 77, 82–5
  and delinquency, 20–21
  defined, 11–12
  through education, 3, 28–32, 46–51
'Streaming' in schools, 29
SOLEYMAN THE MAGNIFICENT, 144
Suffragettes, 50, 126

Tallensi, 137, 139, 148
TANNER, J. M., 156, 158–9, 161–2
Tiv of Nigeria, 79, 140–41
Tonga tribe, 148
Turks, 143–5

Uganda, 128, 129, 130
Uniforms, at grammar schools, 108, 160
Universities
  personality development at, 4–9, 14, 151
  residence, 153–4

Values and education, 9, 151–2

Warrior age-groups, 127, 133, 134, 135, 146–7
WATTS, ISAAC, 52
W.E.A., 152
Winchester College, 48
Wisdom of adults, 15, 150, 163
Wishful-thinking among adults, 14
Witchcraft accusations and inter-generation tension, 135
Women's higher education, 50–51
WOLLESTONECRAFT, MARY, 42, 50

'Young Italy', 125
'Young Turks', 145
Youth clubs, 122–3, 154–5

For Product Safety Concerns and Information please contact our EU
representative GPSR@taylorandfrancis.com
Taylor & Francis Verlag GmbH, Kaufingerstraße 24, 80331 München, Germany

www.ingramcontent.com/pod-product-compliance
Lightning Source LLC
Chambersburg PA
CBHW050716280326
41926CB00088B/3045